Growing in Children's Bulletins

by Linda Standke

Carson-Dellosa Publishing Company, Inc. • Greensboro, North Carolina

It is the mission of Carson-Dellosa to create the highest-quality
Scripture-based children's products that teach the Word of God, share His love
and goodness, assist in faith development, and glorify His Son, Jesus Christ.

"... *teach me your ways so I may know you....*"
Exodus 33:13

Credits

Editors .... Pamela Holley-Bright, Kathie Szitas
Layout Design .... Clint Moore
Inside Illustrations .... Bill Neville
Cover Design .... Peggy Jackson
Cover Illustrations .... Nick Greenwood

Unless otherwise noted, Scripture is taken from the HOLY BIBLE, NEW INTERNATIONAL VERSION®, copyright © 1973, 1978, 1984 by International Bible Society. Used by permission of Zondervan Bible Publishers.

Scripture quotations marked NLT are taken from the *Holy Bible*, New Living Translation, copyright © 1996, 2004. Used by permission of Tyndale House Publishers, Inc., Wheaton, Illinois 60189. All rights reserved.

Scripture quotations marked NIrV are taken from the *Holy Bible*, NEW INTERNATIONAL READER'S VERSION®. Copyright © 1996, 1998 International Bible Society. All rights reserved throughout the world. Used by permission of International Bible Society.

Scripture quotations marked NCV are taken from the *International Children's Bible®, New Century Version®*, Copyright © 1986, 1988, 1999 by Tommy Nelson™, a division of Thomas Nelson, Inc., Nashville, Tennessee 37214. Used by permission.

© 2007, Carson-Dellosa Publishing Company, Inc., Greensboro, North Carolina 27425. The purchase of this material entitles the buyer to reproduce worksheets and activities for classroom use only—not for commercial resale. Reproduction of these materials for an entire school or district is prohibited. No part of this book may be reproduced (except as noted above), stored in a retrieval system, or transmitted in any form or by any means (mechanically, electronically, recording, etc.) without the prior written consent of Carson-Dellosa Publishing Co., Inc.

Printed in the USA · All rights reserved.

ISBN 978-1-59441-293-6
02-146141151

To my four delightful boys: Nicholas, Danny, Tim, and Jeff.
You taught me the value of having quiet activities for children in church.
Your support for my writing and belief in me has meant more than you will ever know.
You have discovered the mystery that is in Christ Jesus and you are now men of integrity.
I am so honored to be your mom and I love you more than you could know.

*Father in Heaven,
I ask that You guide the precious little hands that will
do these puzzles. May there be joy in their hearts that only
comes from You as they learn and grow in Your love and grace.
Amen.*

Grow in the grace of our Lord and Savior Jesus Christ. Get to know him better.
2 Peter 3:18 NIrV

Table of Contents

How to Use This Book 6

How to Make the Children's Bulletins 7

Prepare Your Heart 8

God Made All Things 9

Adam and Eve 11

Noah Becomes an Ark-itect 13

Count the Stars 15

Joseph, the Dreamer 17

God's Man, Moses 19

Joshua's Victory 21

Boy Beats Big Bully 23

Give God Glorious Praise 25

The Bible Is God's Word 27

The Lions That Did Not Roar 29

Jonah's Fish Story 31

God's Angels 33

The Birth Proclaimed 35

A Christmas Journey 37

A King Is Born 39

John the Baptist 41

Jesus Is Baptized 43

The Woman at the Well 45

Calling the Disciples 47

Fishers of Men 49

Jesus, the Healer 51

A Man through the Roof 53

Shine Your Light 55

Ask, Seek, Knock 57

The Sower	59
Jesus Calms the Storm	60
Jesus Feeds 5,000	63
The Miracles of Jesus	65
The Good Samaritan	67
The Lost Sheep	69
The Parable of the Lost Coin	71
Let the Children Come to Me	73
Up a Tree	75
Jesus Is King!	77
Jesus Will Return	79
Jesus Sets the Example	81
A New Command	83
Holy Week	85
The Way to the Father	87
He Is Risen	89
God Gave Us Jesus	91
The Holy Spirit Comes	93
Saul Sees the Light	95
Forgiveness	97
Faith, Hope, and Love	99
A New Creation	101
Saved by Faith	103
Armor of God	105
Give Thanks	107
Talking to God	109
The Alpha and Omega	111

How to Use This Book

Growing in Grace Children's Bulletins contains 52 fun, faith-building bulletins that cover key Old and New Testament stories and themes. Simply remove each page at the perforation. Then, photocopy, fold, and distribute the four-page bulletins for children to enjoy.

Each secret code, hidden picture, maze, and puzzle activity is designed to increase children's knowledge of God's Word and equip them to grow in the grace of the Lord.

Use these bulletins for:

- Worship services
- Take-home Sunday School papers
- Extension activities
- VBS activities
- Early arrivals
- Early finishers
- Outreach tools

These bulletins teach:

- Old Testament stories such as:

    God Made All Things
    Adam and Eve
    Noah Becomes an Ark-itect
    Count the Stars
    Joseph, the Dreamer
    God's Man, Moses
    Joshua's Victory
    Boy Beats Big Bully
    Give God Glorious Praise
    The Lions That Did Not Roar

- New Testament stories such as:

    A Christmas Journey
    Calling the Disciples
    A New Command
    Jesus Will Return
    The Way to the Father
    He Is Risen
    Saul Sees the Light
    A New Creation
    Saved by Faith
    The Alpha and Omega

- Values such as:

    Helping others
    Sharing with others
    Caring for others
    Encouraging others
    Giving to others

- Spiritual concepts such as:

    God made us
    God loves us
    God forgives us
    God hears us
    God is with us

How to Make the Children's Bulletins

There are 52 bulletins in this book. Each bulletin is made from two consecutive pages. For example, the bulletin shown, "Joseph, the Dreamer", is printed from pages 17 and 18. The front and back covers of the bulletin are on page 17, while the inside pages are on page 18. When folded in half, the four-page bulletins will be the same size as a standard church bulletin.

Remove Pages
Carefully separate the page along the perforation. To reduce the risk of tearing, first score the perforation with a craft knife or a scissors tip.

Make a Two-Sided Copy
Use the form feeder and follow the duplexing instructions of your copier. Copies can be enlarged by 2 percent, if desired.

Option
To copy without a form feeder, place the first page of the worship bulletin facedown on the copy machine. Place the non-perforated side of the paper flush with the edge of the copier.

Copy this page once for each child. Then, turn the copies over and put them back into the paper drawer of the copier.

Turn the original page over with the non-perforated side of the paper flush with the edge of the copier.

Copy this page to create a double-sided bulletin.

Fold and Distribute
Fold along the center of each page to make a four-page bulletin. Crayons or colorful pencils will work best when copied onto standard paper. Markers can be used if the bulletins are copied onto heavier paper. Encourage children to take the bulletins home and share their work with their families.

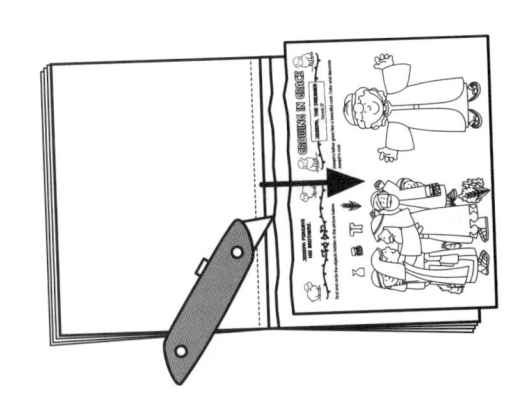

© Carson-Dellosa   Growing in Grace Children's Bulletins • CD-204028

PREPARE YOUR HEART FOR WORSHIP BULLETIN MINISTRY

Whoever accepts a child in my name accepts me.
Matthew 18:5 NCV

Pray for God's guidance and blessings on your Worship Bulletin ministry.

- Ask God to help you choose the right bulletin for the right day. *He will!*
- Ask God to prepare the hearts of the children to understand and receive God's Word. *He will!*
- Ask God to give you encouraging words as you distribute the worship bulletins. *He will!*
- Ask God to bless each child who receives a bulletin. *He will!*

Use the Scriptures below to prepare your own heart and to pray for children's understanding as they learn God's Word through the *Growing in Grace Children's Bulletins*.

. . . since the day we heard about you, we have not stopped praying for you and asking God to fill you with the knowledge of his will through all spiritual wisdom and understanding. And we pray this in order that you may live a life worthy of the Lord and may please him in every way: bearing fruit in every good work, growing in the knowledge of God.

Colossians 1:9–10

I keep asking that the God of our Lord Jesus Christ, the glorious Father, may give you the Spirit of wisdom and revelation, so that you may know him better. I pray also that the eyes of your heart may be enlightened in order that you may know the hope to which he has called you, the riches of his glorious inheritance in the saints, and his incomparably great power for us who believe.

Ephesians 1:17–19

I pray that out of his glorious riches he may strengthen you with power through his Spirit in your inner being, so that Christ may dwell in your hearts through faith. And I pray that you, being rooted and established in love, may have power, together with all the saints, to grasp how wide and long and high and deep is the love of Christ, and to know this love that surpasses knowledge—that you may be filled to the measure of all the fullness of God.

Ephesians 3:16–19

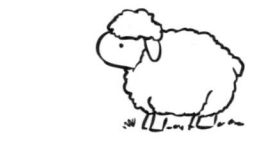

GROWING IN GRACE

GOD MADE ALL THINGS
Genesis 1

God made all of the fish in the sea. Draw lines to connect the matching fish.

GOD MADE YOU!

Draw and color the person below to look just like you!

Growing in Grace Children's Bulletins • CD-204028

© Carson-Dellosa

GOD MADE THE ANIMALS.

Circle the animals hidden in the picture below.

cat   horse   rabbit   sheep   duck

GOD MADE PLANTS FOR US TO EAT.

Color and count the apples on the tree below. Then, circle the number of apples in the tree.

4   6   7   9

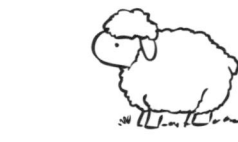

GROWING IN GRACE

ADAM AND EVE
Genesis 2

God made man. Trace the dotted lines. Then, draw Adam's eyes, nose, and mouth.

GOD MADE A HELPER FOR ADAM.

Find and circle the objects hidden in the picture below.

Growing in Grace Children's Bulletins • CD-204028

© Carson-Dellosa

GOD MADE A BEAUTIFUL GARDEN.

Find the name of the garden by following the vines from each letter to the flower. Then, write the letter on the line below.

D   N   E   N   E   E

_ _ _ _ _ _

ADAM NAMED THE ANIMALS.

Trace the line to connect each animal to its name.

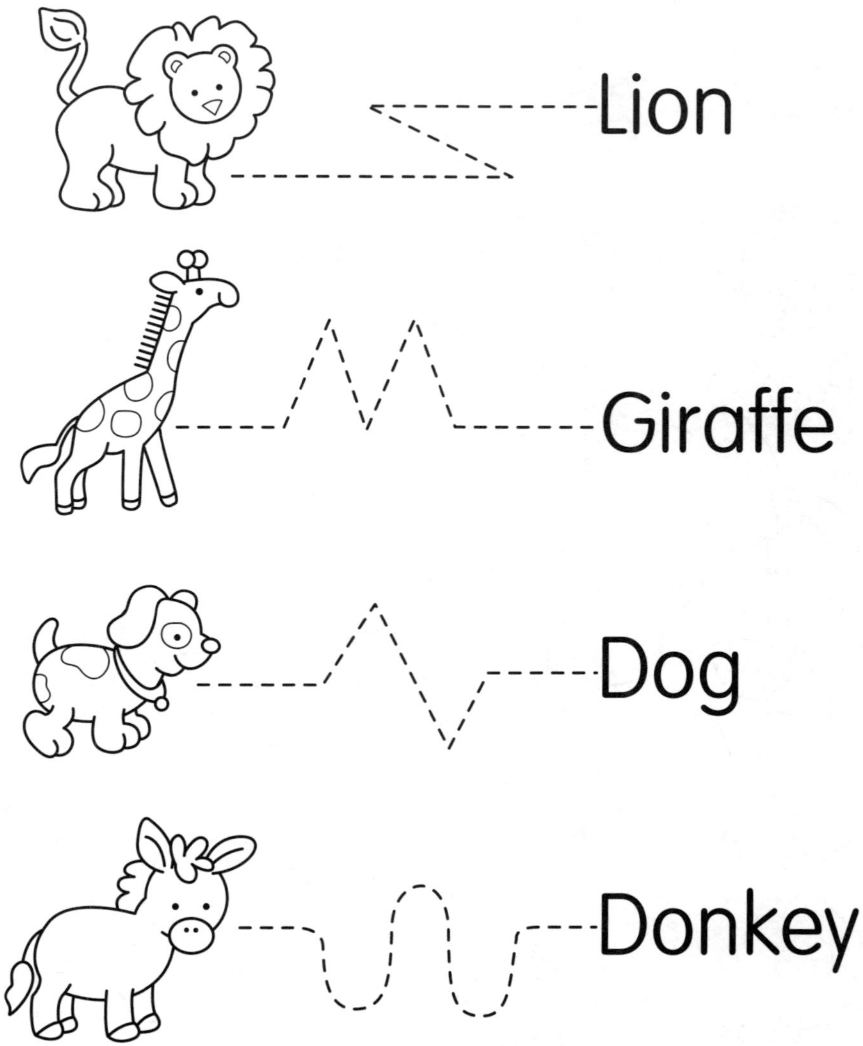

Lion

Giraffe

Dog

Donkey

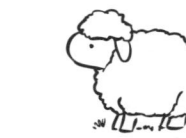

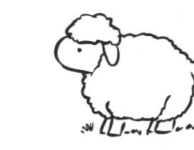

GROWING IN GRACE

GIVE GOD GLORIOUS PRAISE
Psalm 66:1–2

Match the numbers with the letters. Then, write the letters on the lines to find out one way that God likes for us to praise Him.

S _ _ _ _
2 4 9 5 7

_ _ _ _
6 3 7 4

_ _ _ !
8 9 1

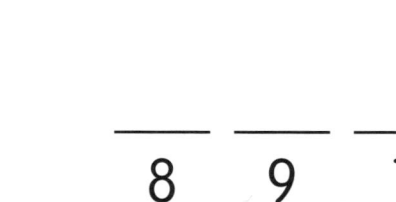

Y	S	I	H	U	W	T	J	O
1	2	3	4	5	6	7	8	9

© Carson-Dellosa   Growing in Grace Children's Bulletins • CD-204028

ALL OF THE EARTH, SHOUT WITH JOY!

To whom should you shout with joy? Trace the lines to find out. Then, color the picture.

THE ANIMALS PRAISE GOD, TOO!

Match each animal to a megaphone by tracing the dotted lines.

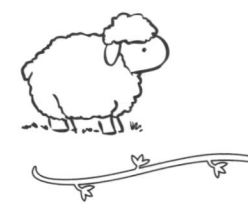

SHOUT WITH JOY EVERY DAY.

Color the banner.

SHOUT WITH JOY!

GROWING IN GRACE

THE BIBLE IS GOD'S WORD
Psalm 119:11

God wants us to remember His Word by keeping it in our hearts. Trace the letters, then color the heart.

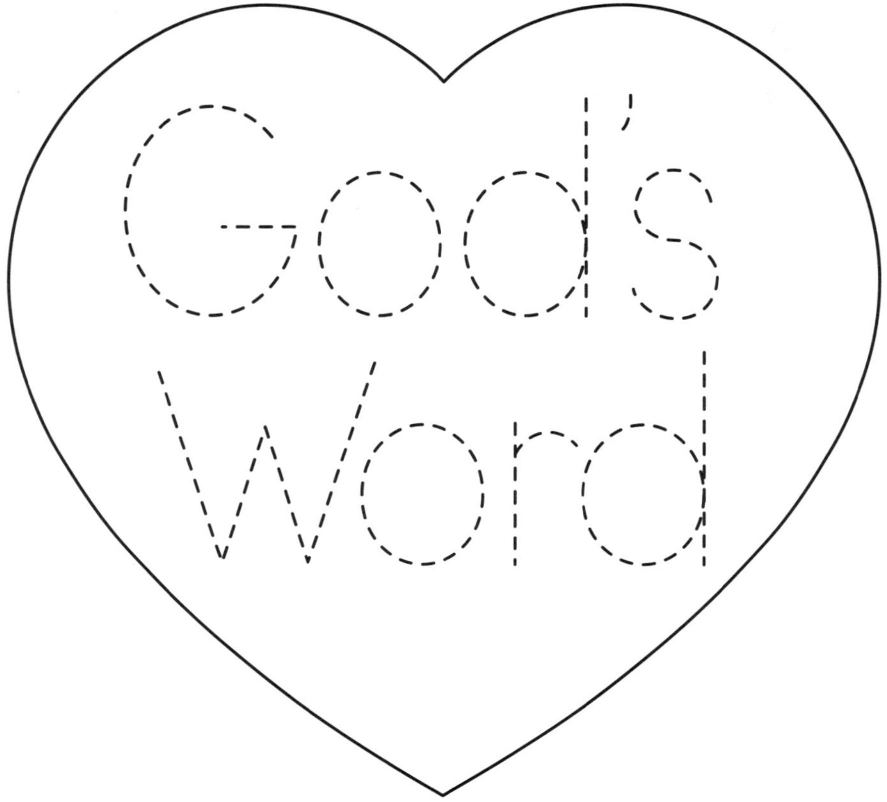

THE BIBLE COMES FROM GOD.

Connect the dots A–V to see where we find God's Word.

GOD'S WORD STANDS FOREVER.

Finish the sentence by following the paths from each letter to the line. Then, write the letter on the line below.

The word of God stands

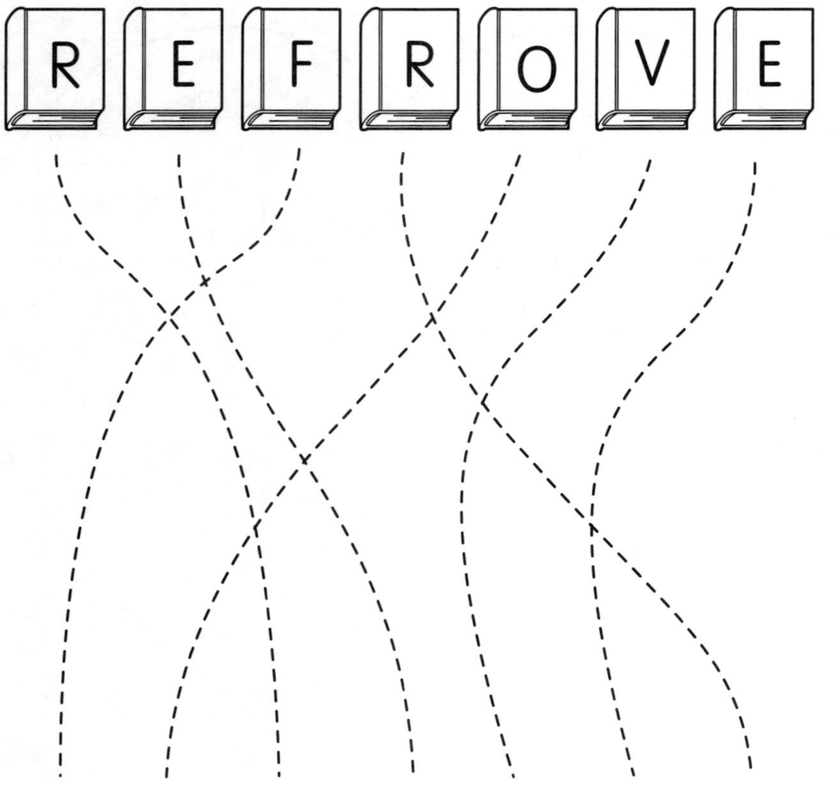

R E F R O V E

_ _ _ _ _ _ _ .

GOD'S WORD IS A LAMP THAT GUIDES US.

Follow the maze to help the child find Jesus.

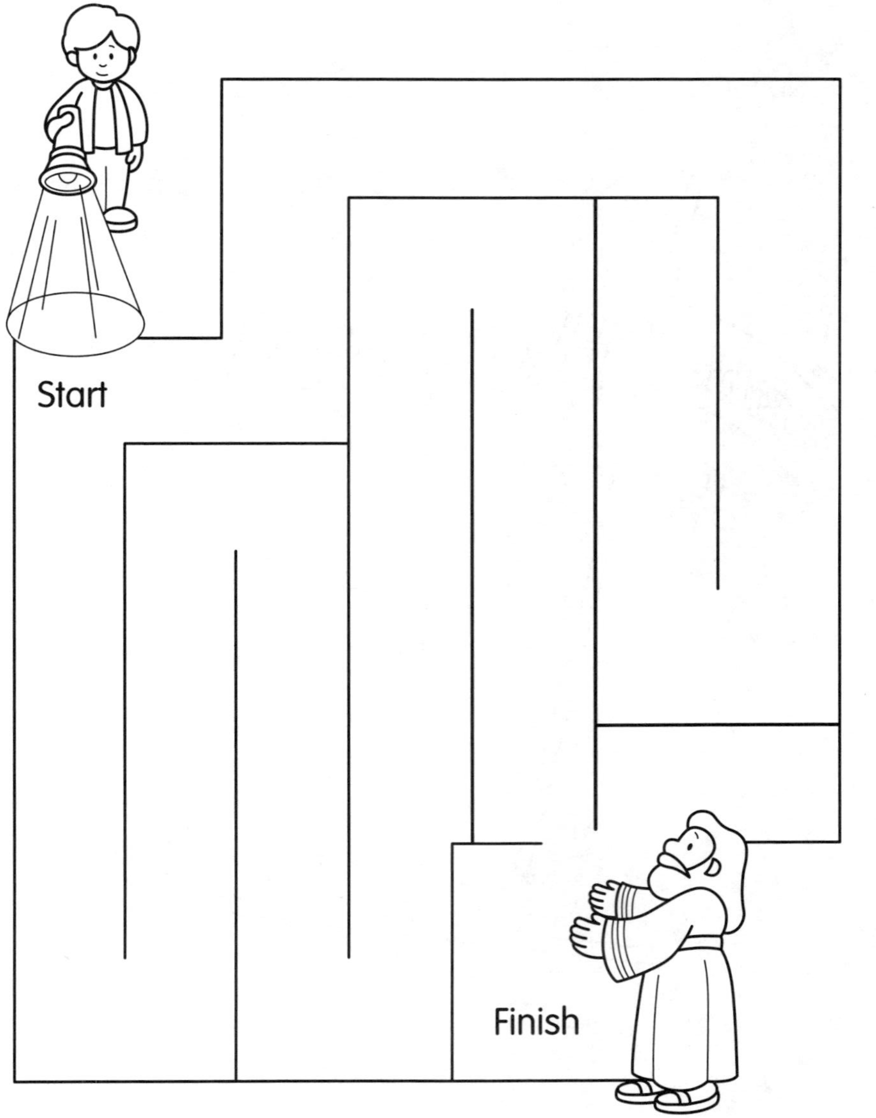

Start

Finish

GROWING IN GRACE

THE LIONS THAT DID NOT ROAR
Daniel 6

Daniel worshiped only the one true God. What did Daniel continue to do even though it was against the law? To find out, follow the paths from each letter to the line. Then, write the letters on the lines.

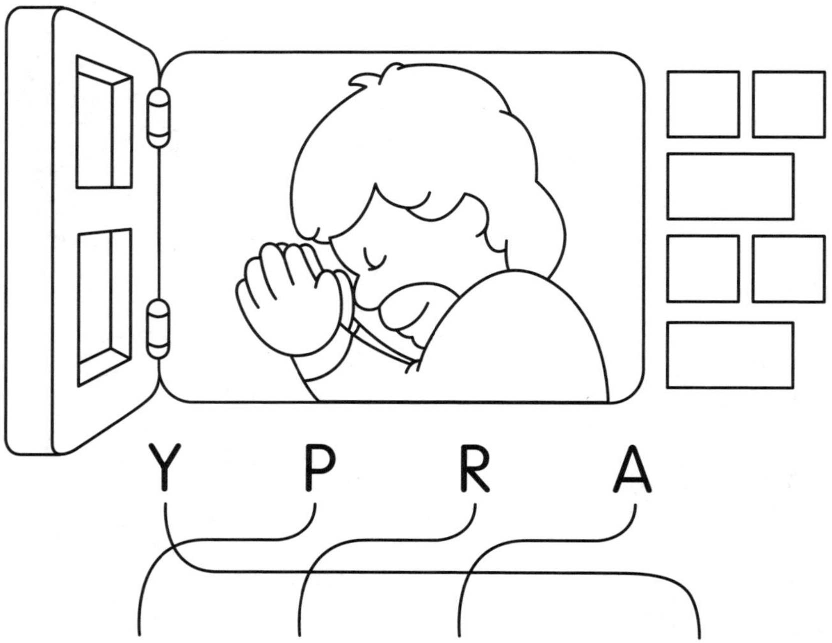

Y   P   R   A

KING DARIUS WORSHIPED GOD.

King Darius made a new law. It said that everyone must worship Daniel's God. Connect the dots A–Z.

© Carson-Dellosa

Growing in Grace Children's Bulletins • CD-204028

DANIEL WAS THROWN INTO THE LIONS' DEN.

Circle the two lions that are the same.

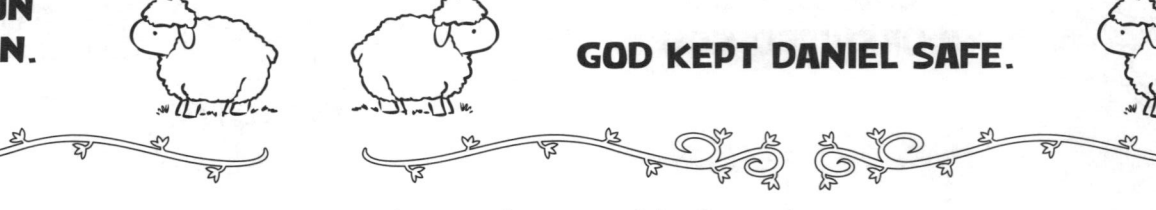

GOD KEPT DANIEL SAFE.

Help Daniel get out of the lions' den.

Start

Finish

GROWING IN GRACE

JONAH'S FISH STORY
Jonah 1–2

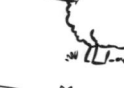

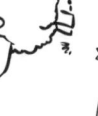

Jonah did not want to do what God told him. He tried to run away from God. Find and circle Jonah sleeping in the boat.

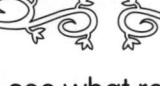

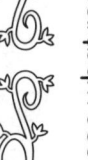

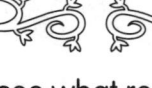

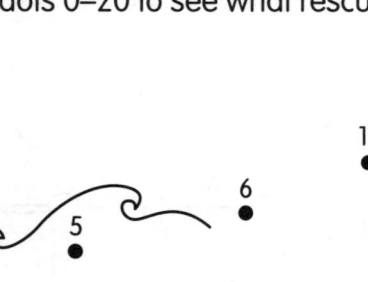

THE FISH SPIT JONAH ONTO DRY LAND.

Connect the dots 0–20 to see what rescued Jonah.

© Carson-Dellosa

Growing in Grace Children's Bulletins • CD-204028

JONAH PRAYED TO GOD.

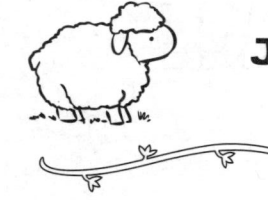

Count and circle the number of pairs of praying hands in each row.

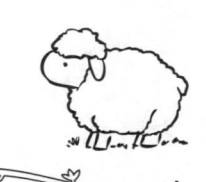

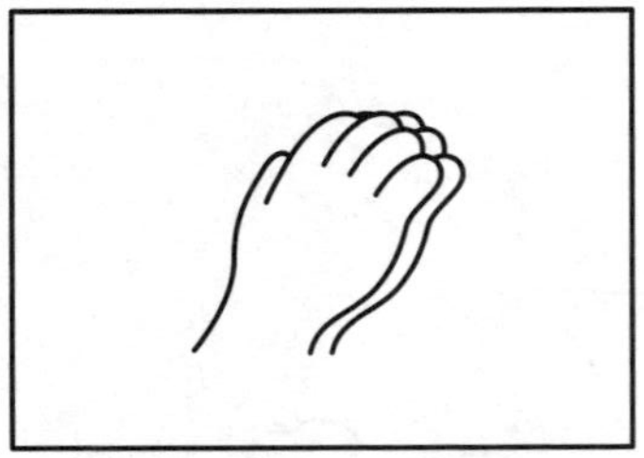

1 2 3
3 4 5 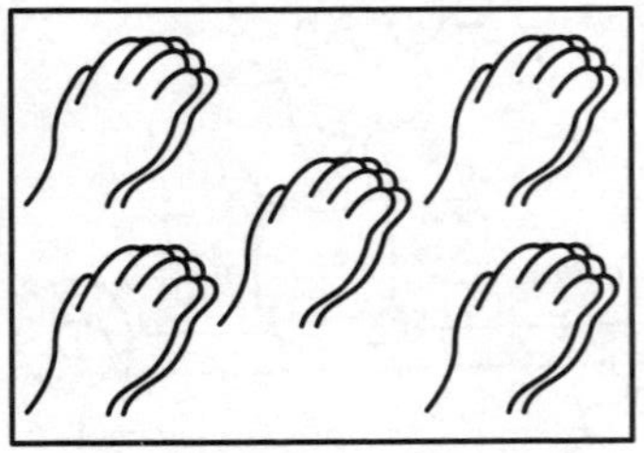
1 2 3 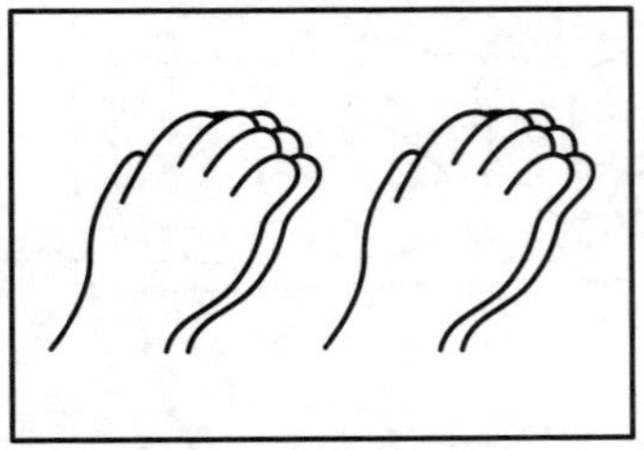
3 4 5 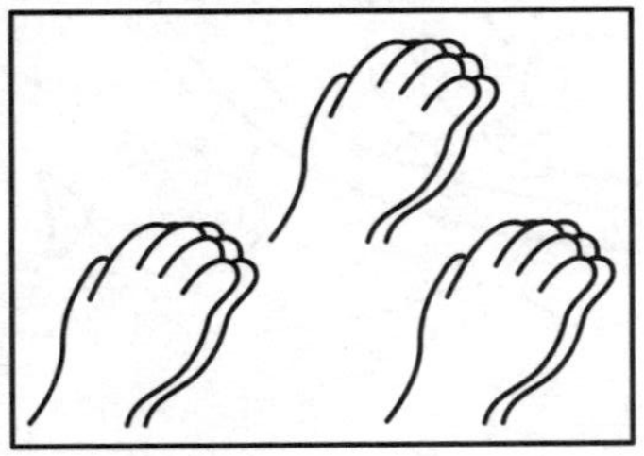

GOD SENT A BIG FISH TO RESCUE JONAH.

Follow the line from each boat. Then, circle the Jonah who ends up in the belly of the fish.

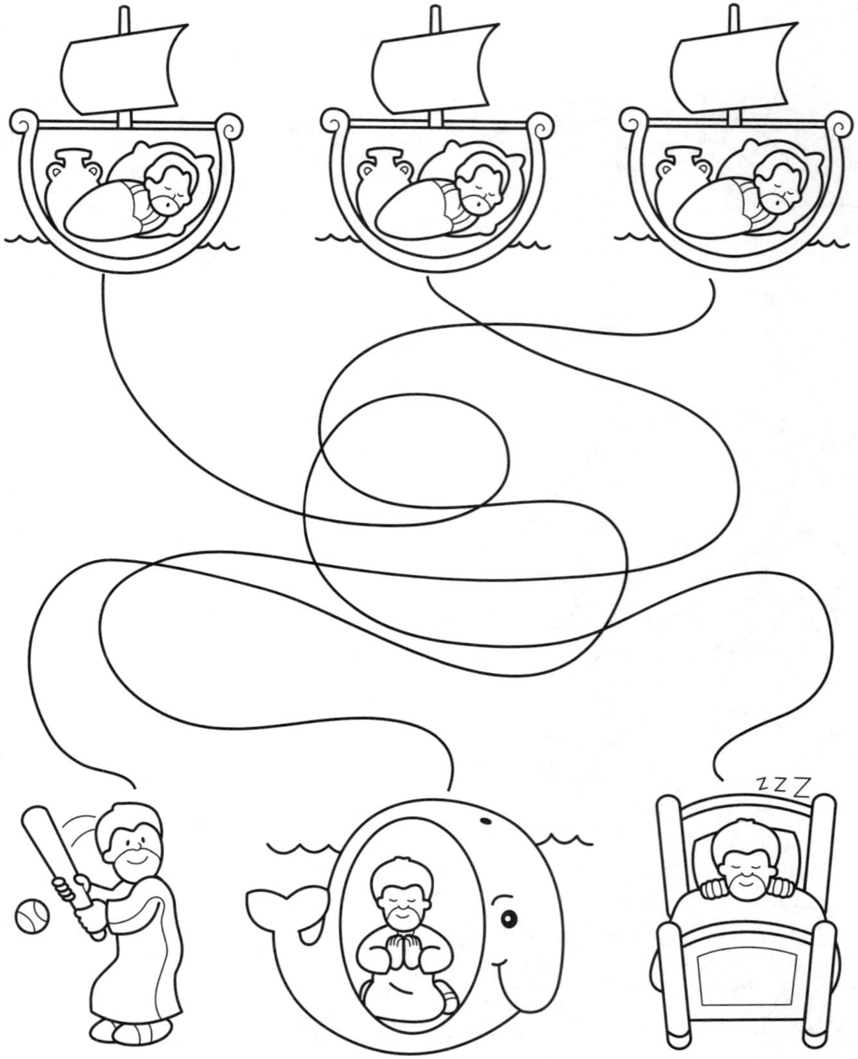

GROWING IN GRACE

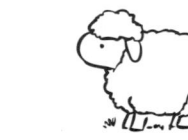

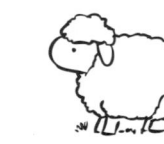

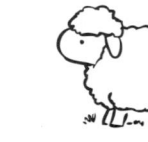

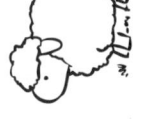

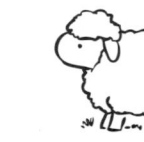

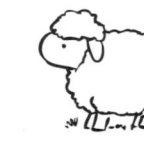

GOD'S ANGELS
Luke 1:26–33; Matthew 1:20–25

An angel told a young woman that she would have a special baby. Match the pictures. Then, write each letter on the line below to find out her name.

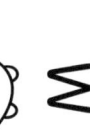

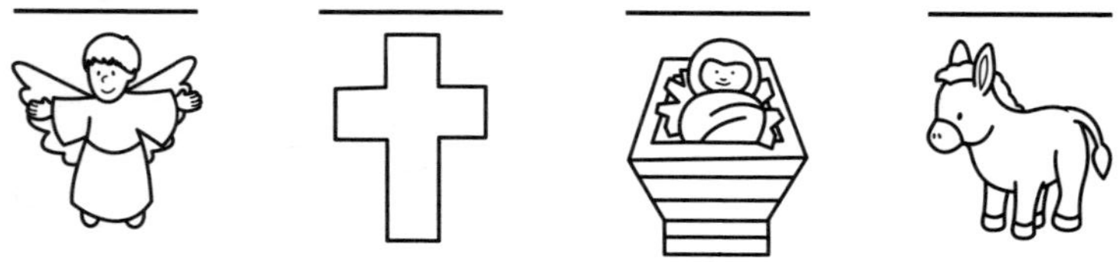

GOD'S ANGELS ARE SPECIAL MESSENGERS.

Circle the two angels that are the same.

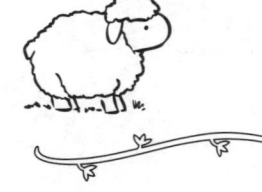

JOSEPH HEARD A SPECIAL MESSAGE.

Beginning at the star, connect the dots A–Z to see who came to Joseph in a dream.

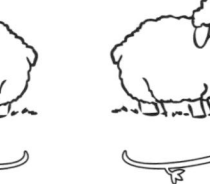

GOD NAMES HIS SON.

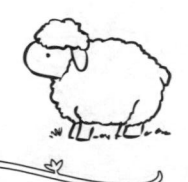

God's angel told Mary and Joseph what to name their baby. His name means "God is with us."
Color the shapes that have a ★ red.
Color the shapes that have a ● green.

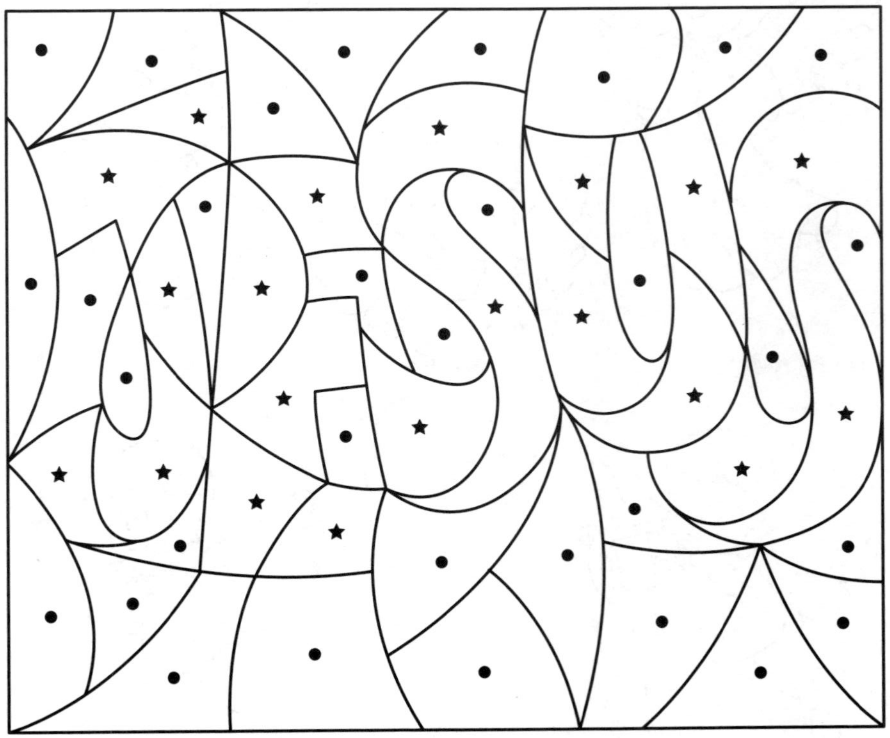

GROWING IN GRACE

THE BIRTH PROCLAIMED
Luke 2; Matthew 2

The shepherds were watching their sheep when an angel told them the news that a King was born. Circle the three lambs hidden in the picture.

JESUS WAS BORN FOR EVERYONE.

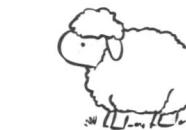

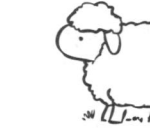

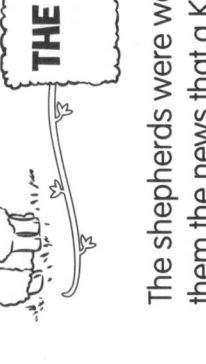

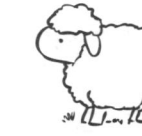

Put the pictures in order by drawing a line from the number to the picture.

1

2

3

4

Growing in Grace Children's Bulletins • CD-204028

© Carson-Dellosa

THE WISE MEN FOLLOWED A STAR TO FIND THE NEW KING.

Count and circle the number of stars in each box.

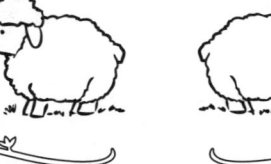

1 2 3

2 3 4

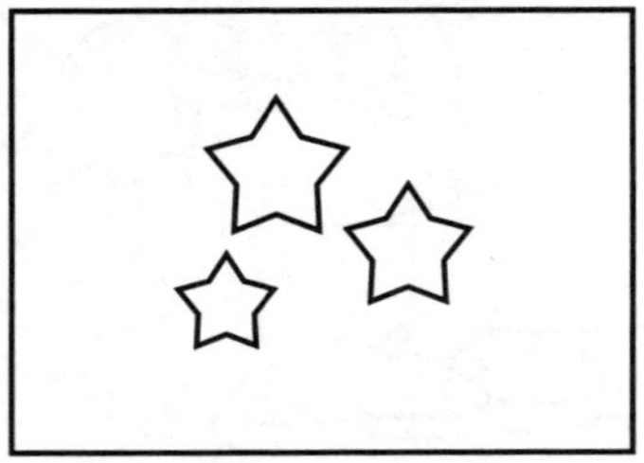

3 4 5

THE WISE MEN BROUGHT GIFTS TO JESUS.

Draw lines connecting each wise man to the matching gift.

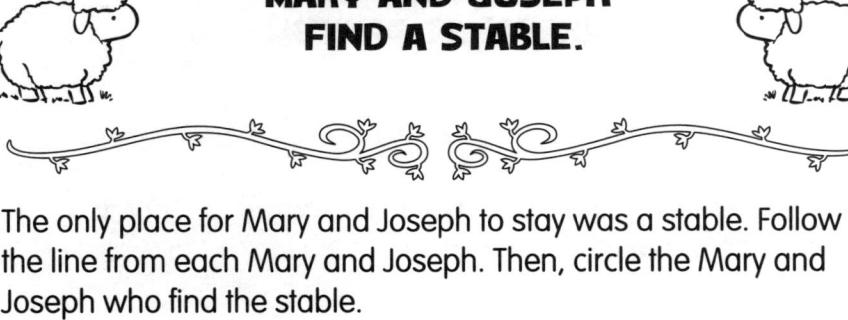

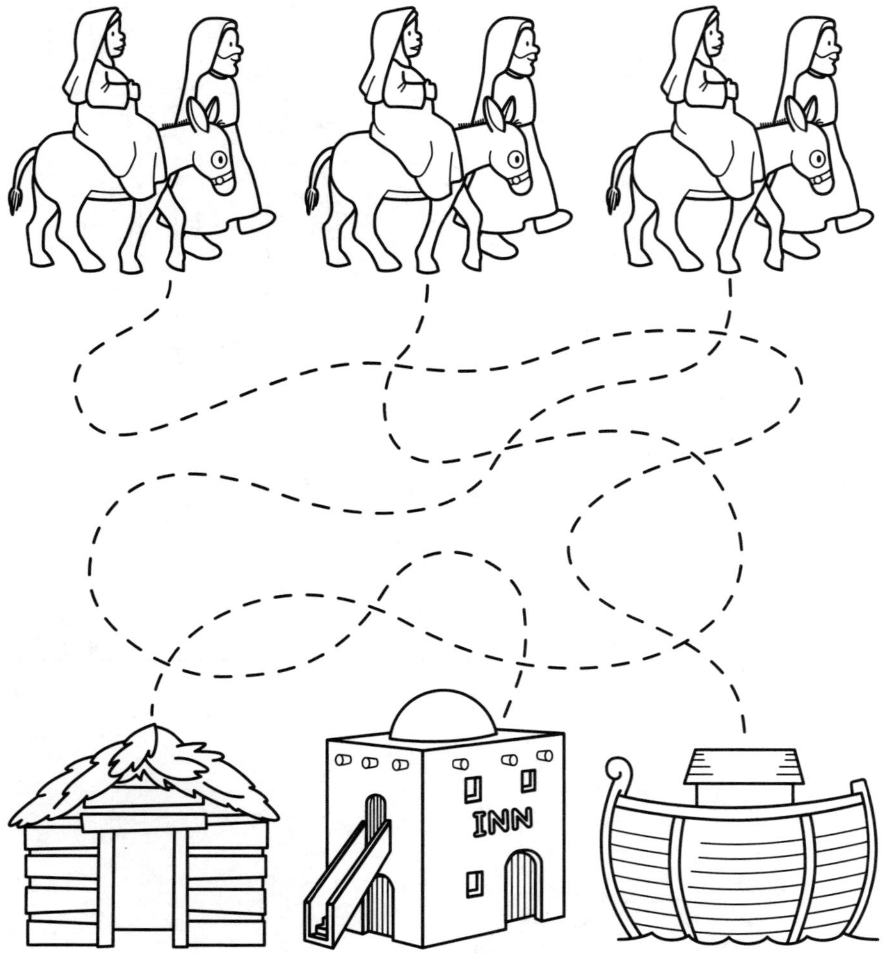

GROWING IN GRACE

A CHRISTMAS JOURNEY
Luke 2

Mary and Joseph traveled to Bethlehem. Help Mary and Joseph find the stable.

Start

Finish

MARY AND JOSEPH FIND A STABLE.

The only place for Mary and Joseph to stay was a stable. Follow the line from each Mary and Joseph. Then, circle the Mary and Joseph who find the stable.

MARY AND JOSEPH GO TO BETHLEHEM.

Mary was expecting a child and rode an animal on her journey to Bethlehem. Connect the dots 0–25 to find out what the animal was.

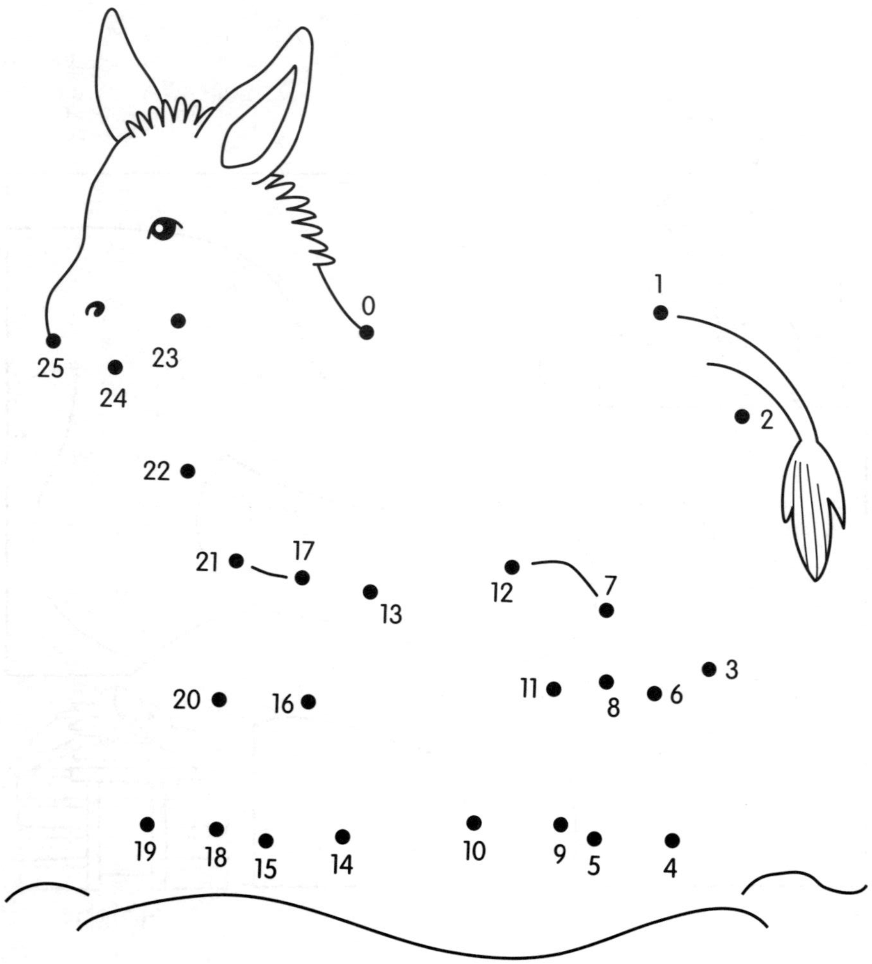

MARY AND JOSEPH ARRIVE AT AN INN.

Write the letter O on the blank lines to find out what Mary and Joseph discovered when they arrived at the inn.

There was  _ _ n _ r _ _ m.

GROWING IN GRACE

A KING IS BORN
Luke 2; Matthew 2

Jesus came to Earth to be our King. Connect the dots 0–12.

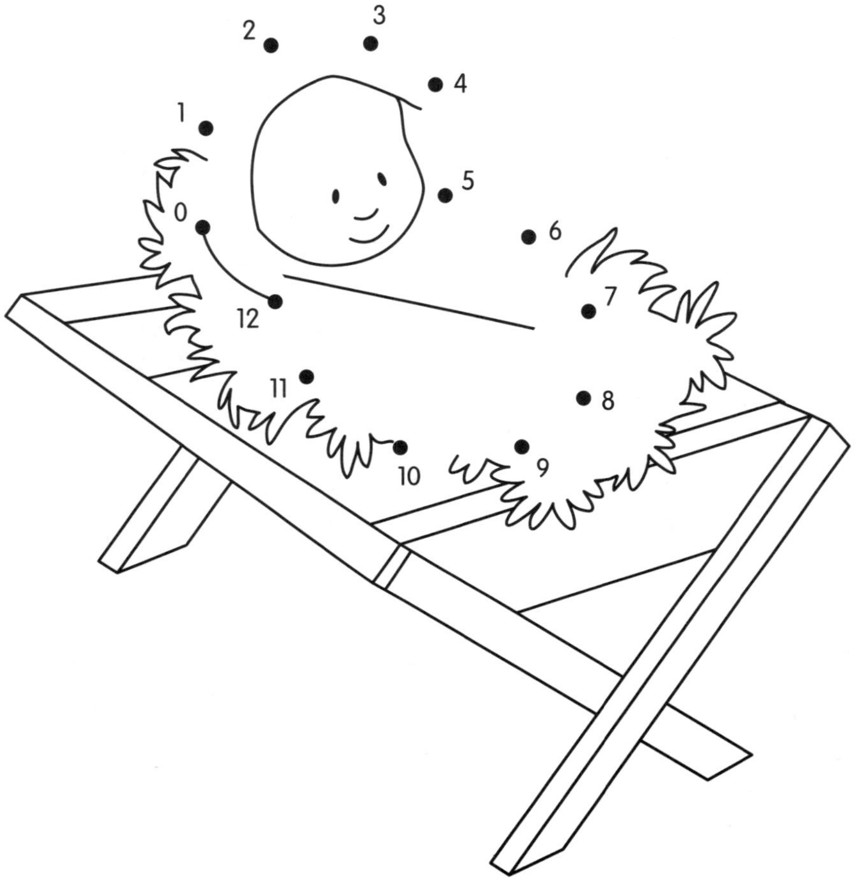

SHEPHERDS AND WISE MEN CAME TO SEE THE NEW KING.

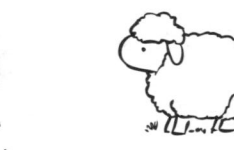

Draw a line to connect each pair of pictures that belong together.

Growing in Grace Children's Bulletins • CD-204028

© Carson-Dellosa

Trace the letters to spell the name of Mary's child.

J E S U S

THE KING'S NAME MEANS "GOD IS WITH US."

Find and circle the objects hidden in the picture below.

MARY PLACED JESUS IN A MANGER.

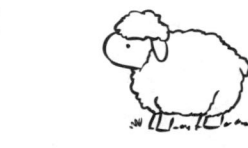

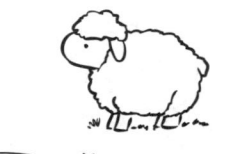

GROWING IN GRACE

JOHN THE BAPTIST
Matthew 3:1–12

John preached in the desert. Connect the dots 0–10.

JOHN PREPARED THE WAY FOR JESUS.

John told people to repent of their sins. Draw a line to connect each matching pair.

JOHN ATE LOCUSTS AND WILD HONEY.

Draw a picture on the dinner plate of foods that you like to eat.

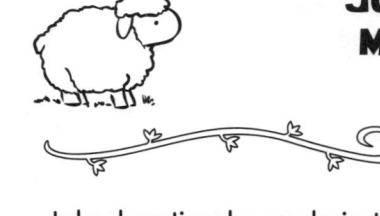

JOHN BAPTIZED MANY PEOPLE.

John baptized people in the Jordan River. Find and circle the objects hidden in the picture below.

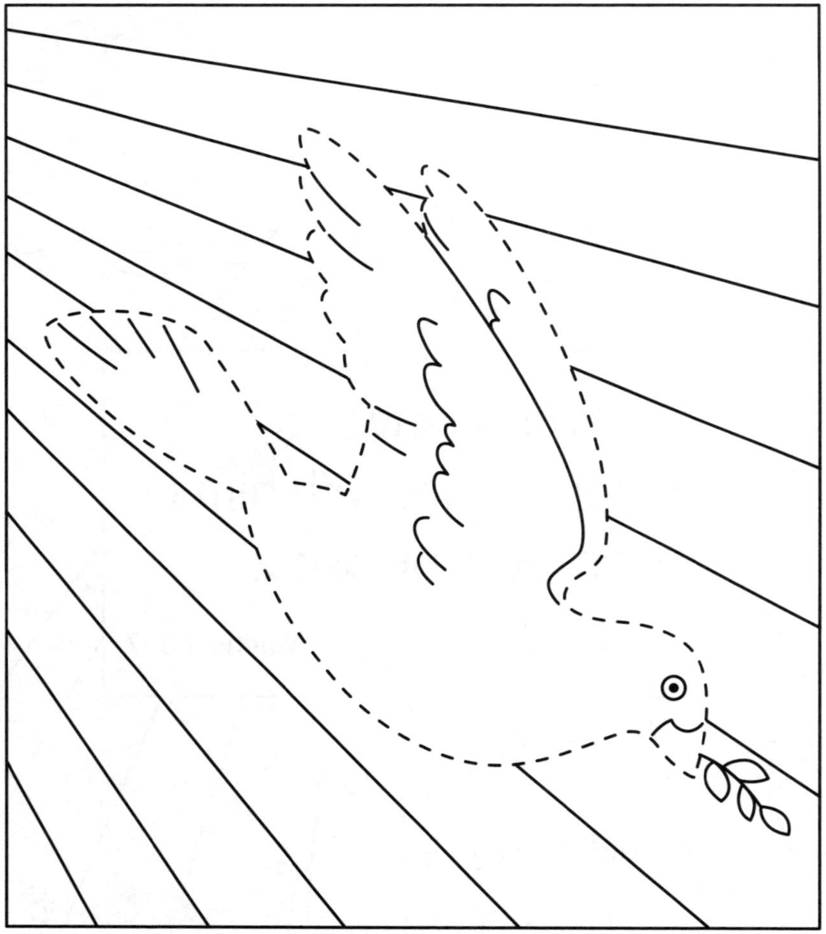

GROWING IN GRACE

JESUS IS BAPTIZED
Matthew 3:13–17

Jesus asked John to baptize Him. Connect the dots 0–26.

THE SPIRIT OF GOD CAME UPON JESUS.

The Spirit of God came down like a dove. Trace the dotted line to draw the dove.

Growing in Grace Children's Bulletins • CD-204028

© Carson-Dellosa

JESUS WAS BAPTIZED IN THE JORDAN RIVER.

Find and circle the objects hidden in the picture below.

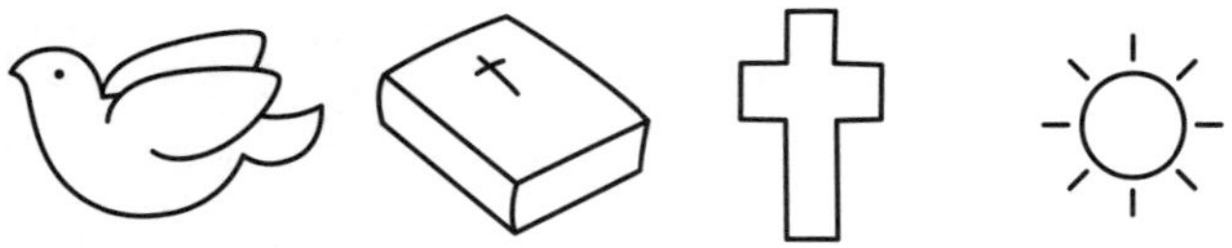

HEAVEN OPENED, AND A VOICE WAS HEARD.

When Jesus was baptized, He heard the Spirit of God speak. Color the picture below.

"This is my Son, whom I love; with him I am well pleased."

Matthew 3:17

GROWING IN GRACE

THE WOMAN AT THE WELL
John 4:1–28

Jesus walked to a town in Samaria and sat by a well. Connect the dots 0–15.

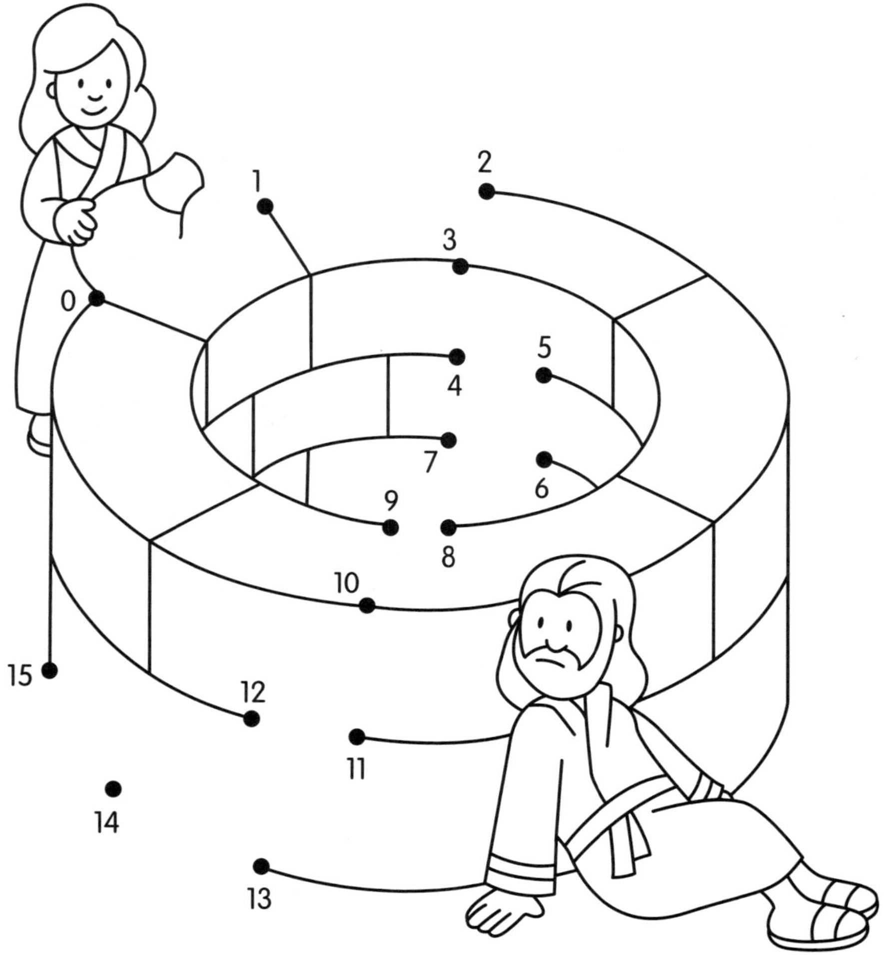

THE WOMAN TOLD HER FRIENDS ABOUT JESUS.

After the woman talked to Jesus, she went back to town to tell her friends. Help the woman find her friends.

JESUS ASKED THE WOMAN FOR SOMETHING.

When a woman came to the well, Jesus asked her a question. Follow each path from the letters to the line. Then, write the letters on the line below to see what Jesus asked.

Jesus asked for a

N R K D I

_ _ _ _ _

THE WOMAN LEARNED HOW TO WORSHIP GOD.

Trace the letters to write how we should worship God.

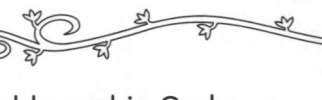

IN SPIRIT AND TRUTH

GROWING IN GRACE

CALLING THE DISCIPLES
Matthew 4:18–22

Simon and Andrew were casting their nets when Jesus walked by. Jesus told them to follow Him. And they did. Connect the dots 0–10.

© Carson-Dellosa

JESUS SAID HE WOULD MAKE THE DISCIPLES FISHERS OF MEN.

Jesus wants you to be a fisher of men, too. Follow each line. Then, circle the child who caught people for Jesus.

Growing in Grace Children's Bulletins • CD-204028

WHEN JESUS CALLED THE MEN, THEY FOLLOWED HIM.

Then Jesus saw James and John who were also fishing. Jesus told them to follow Him. And they did. Help James and John get to Jesus.

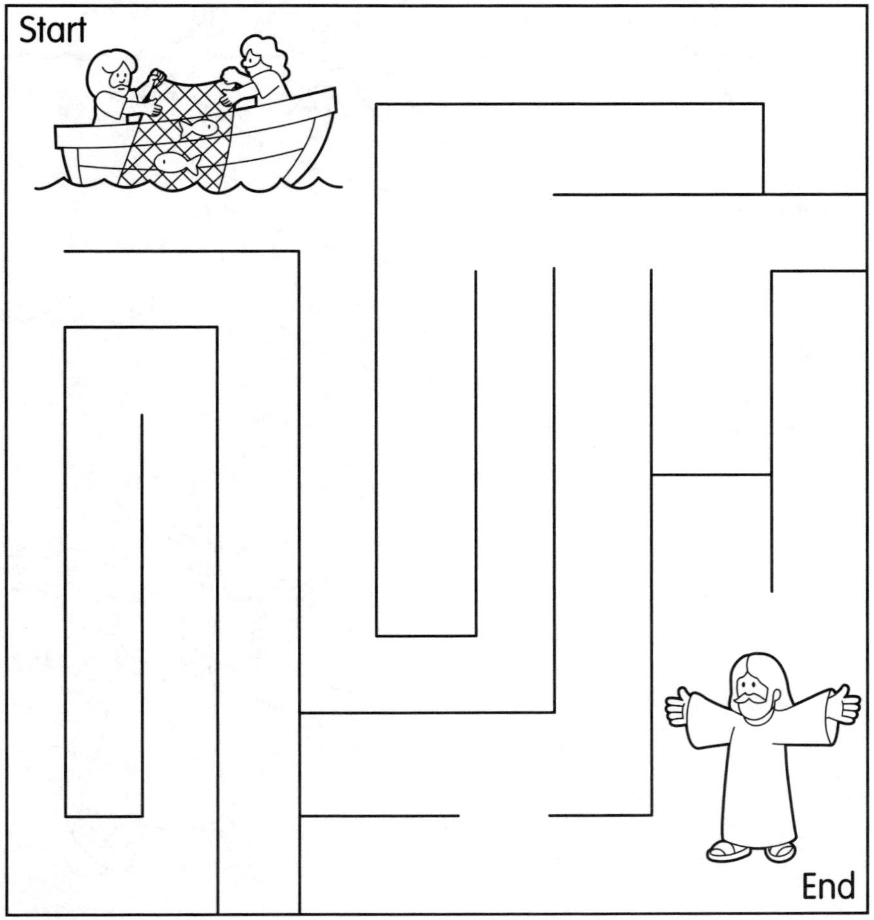

Start

End

YOU CAN FOLLOW JESUS EVERY DAY.

Color all of the shapes that have a 🐟 to see what Jesus said.

Jesus said, "Come, me."

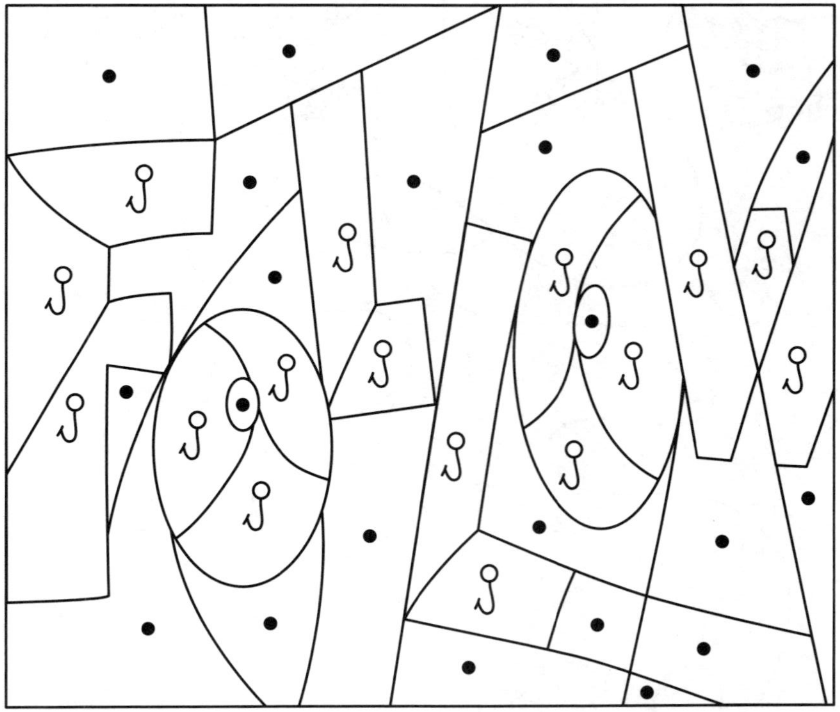

Matthew 4:19

GROWING IN GRACE

FISHERS OF MEN
Mark 1:17

Jesus said, "Follow me, and I will make you fishers of men." Trace the dotted line from each fishing pole to the fish below.

JESUS WANTS YOU TO BE A FISHER OF MEN, TOO.

Following Jesus makes you a fisher of men, too. Match the numbers with the letters to the numbered lines below. Then, write the letters on the lines to find out what Jesus said.

3	4	5	6	7	8
E	F	L	O	M	W

Jesus said,

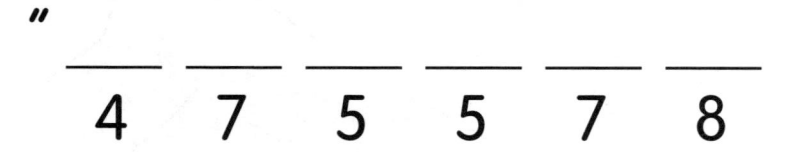

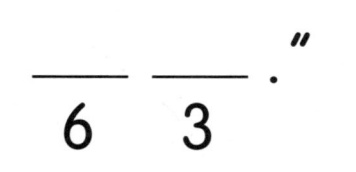

"_ _ _ _ _ _
 4 7 5 5 7 8

 _ _ ."
 6 3

Mark 1:17

FOLLOWING JESUS HELPS OTHERS SEE GOD'S LOVE.

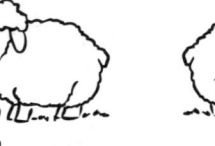

When we share God's love with others, we are fishers of men. Draw an X on the item that does not belong with the other items in the net.

JESUS WANTS US TO TELL OTHERS ABOUT HIS LOVE.

Help the kids find the others so that they can tell them about Jesus.

Start

Finish

GROWING IN GRACE

JESUS, THE HEALER
Luke 17:11–19

Jesus healed 10 men who were very sick. Circle the group of 10 men.

JESUS HEALED MANY PEOPLE.
Luke 4:40

Jesus healed all who came to him. Count and circle the number of people in each row.

4 1 3

6 7 2

5 2 6

© Carson-Dellosa

Growing in Grace Children's Bulletins • CD-204028

A MAN BORN BLIND COULD SEE.
John 9:1-6

Jesus healed a blind man. Connect the dots 0–20.

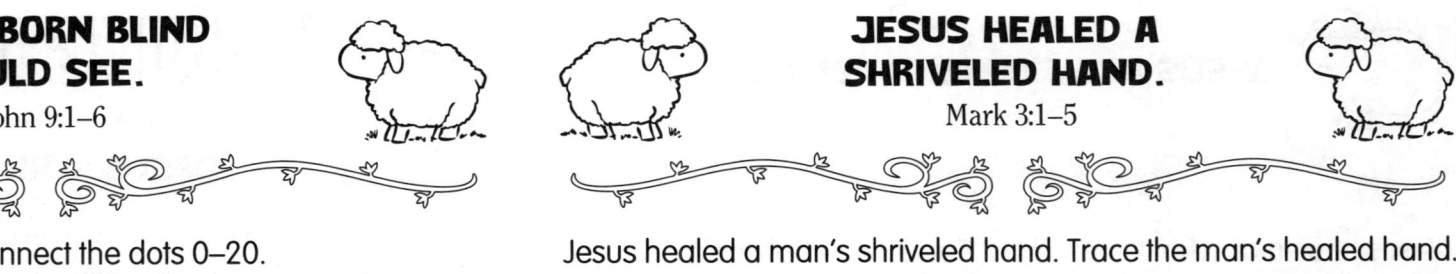

JESUS HEALED A SHRIVELED HAND.
Mark 3:1-5

Jesus healed a man's shriveled hand. Trace the man's healed hand.

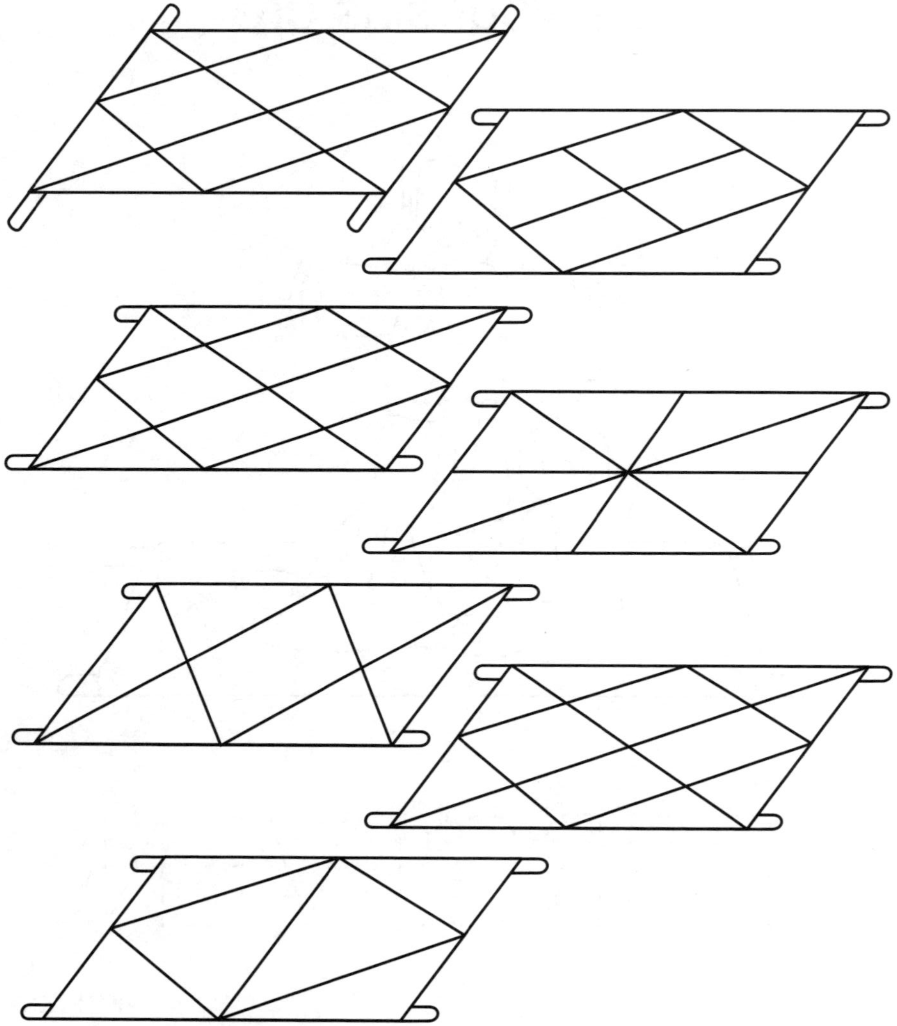

GROWING IN GRACE

A MAN THROUGH THE ROOF
Mark 2:1–5; Matthew 9:6

Some men brought a friend who could not walk to see Jesus. Connect the dots 1–10.

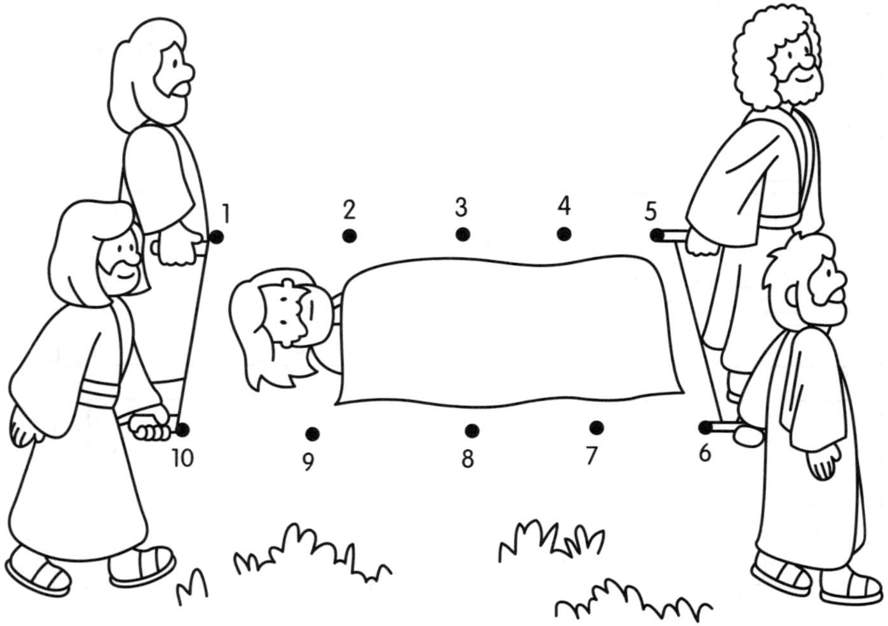

JESUS TOLD THE MAN TO TAKE HIS MAT AND GO HOME.

Jesus healed the man. Circle the two mats that are the same.

THEY LOWERED THEIR FRIEND THROUGH THE ROOF.

It was so crowded that the men could not get near Jesus. Trace the dotted lines to help the men lower their friend from the roof.

JESUS TOLD THE MAN THAT HIS SINS WERE FORGIVEN.

Trace the letters to find out what Jesus said when He saw the man's faith.

"Son, your sins are FORGIVEN."

Mark 2:5

GROWING IN GRACE

SHINE YOUR LIGHT
Matthew 5:14–16

Shine your light by praising God. Draw the other half of the person praising God. Then, decorate the person to look like you.

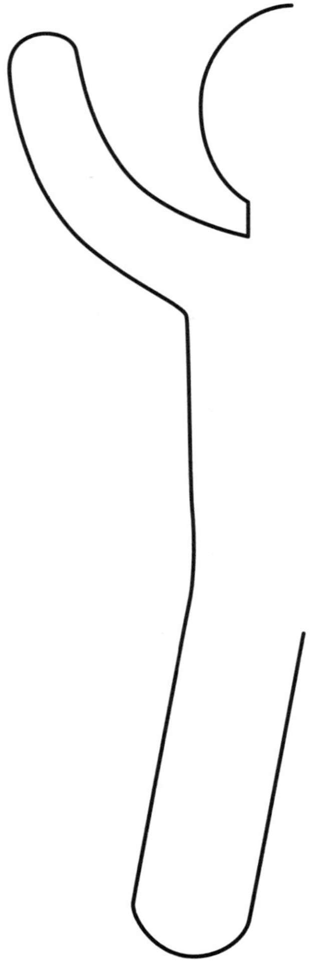

LET YOUR LIGHT SHINE BEFORE MEN.

Circle the light that is different in each row.

DO NOT HIDE YOUR LIGHT.

Let everyone see your light! Find and circle four 🕯 hidden in the picture.

A CITY ON A HILL CANNOT BE HIDDEN.

Jesus wants our light to shine like a city on a hill. Connect the dots 0–23 to see the city on the hill.

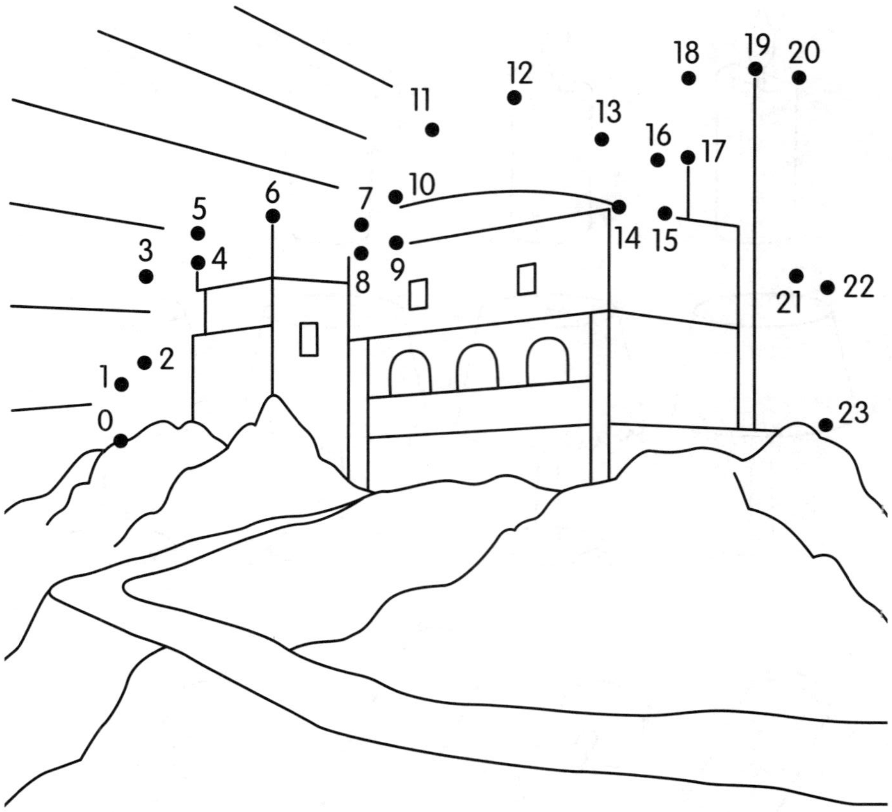

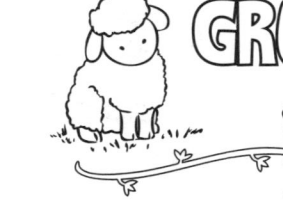

GROWING IN GRACE

ASK, SEEK, KNOCK
Matthew 7:7–8

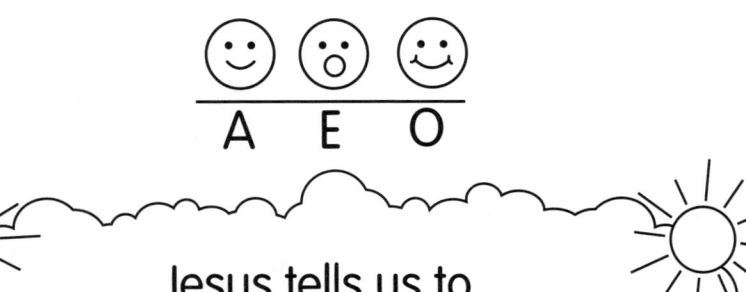

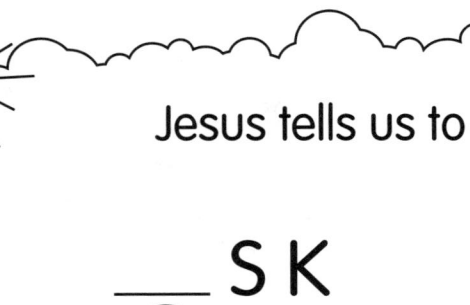

Match the pictures to the letters. Then, write the letters on the lines to read what Jesus tells us we should do.

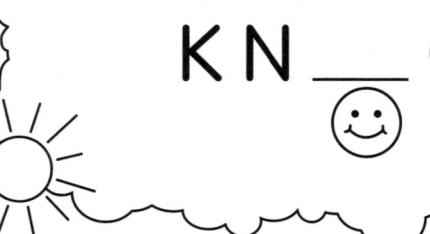

Jesus tells us to

_ S K

S _ _ K AND

K N _ C K.

KNOCK, AND THE DOOR WILL BE OPENED.

Jesus will open the door. Connect the dots 0–6.

ASK AND IT WILL BE GIVEN TO YOU.

Color the shapes with a • to read what Jesus tells us we are to do.

SEEK AND YOU WILL FIND.

Jesus tells us that anyone who seeks Him, will find Him. Find and color the letters in the word SEEK.

58

GROWING IN GRACE

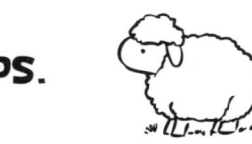

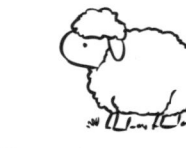

THE SOWER
Matthew 13:1-23

A farmer went outside to sow his seed. Draw a line to connect each matching pair.

THE GOOD SOIL PRODUCED GOOD CROPS.

Color the letters in the word *HEARS* hidden in the corn. Then, trace the letters below to complete the message.

The good soil is like the person who HEARS and understands God's Word.

Growing in Grace Children's Bulletins • CD-204028
© Carson-Dellosa

SOME SEEDS WERE EATEN BY BIRDS.

The seeds that fell on the ground were quickly eaten by birds. Count how many birds are eating seeds along the path. Then, circle the correct number below.

1   2   3   4   5

SOME SEEDS WERE SCORCHED BY THE SUN.

Some seeds dried up in the sun because they did not have any roots. Connect the dots 1–20.

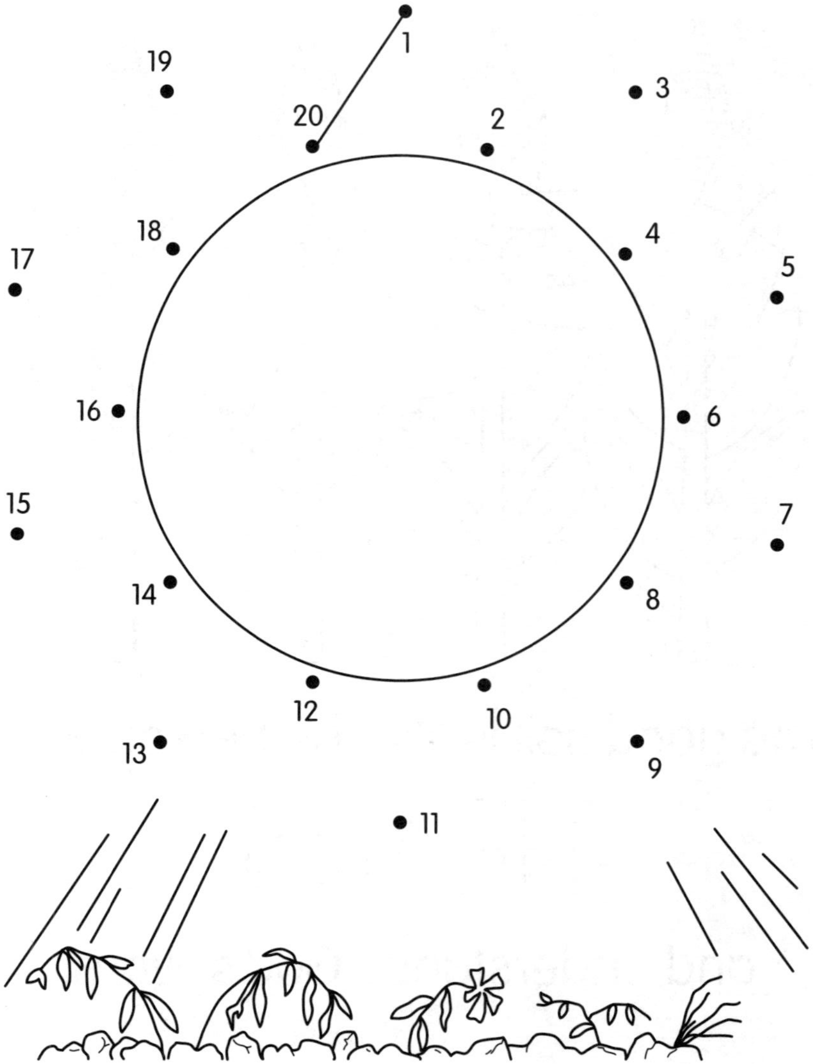

GROWING IN GRACE

JESUS CALMS THE STORM
Matthew 8:23-27

Jesus and the disciples got into the boat. Connect the dots A–X.

EVEN THE WINDS AND THE WAVES OBEYED JESUS.

Jesus told the wind and the waves to be quiet. Then, it was calm. Draw a line to connect each pair of pictures that belong together.

© Carson-Dellosa

Growing in Grace Children's Bulletins • CD-204028

A STORM CAME, AND WAVES SWEPT OVER THE BOAT.

Waves rocked the boat. Trace the dotted lines to complete the picture.

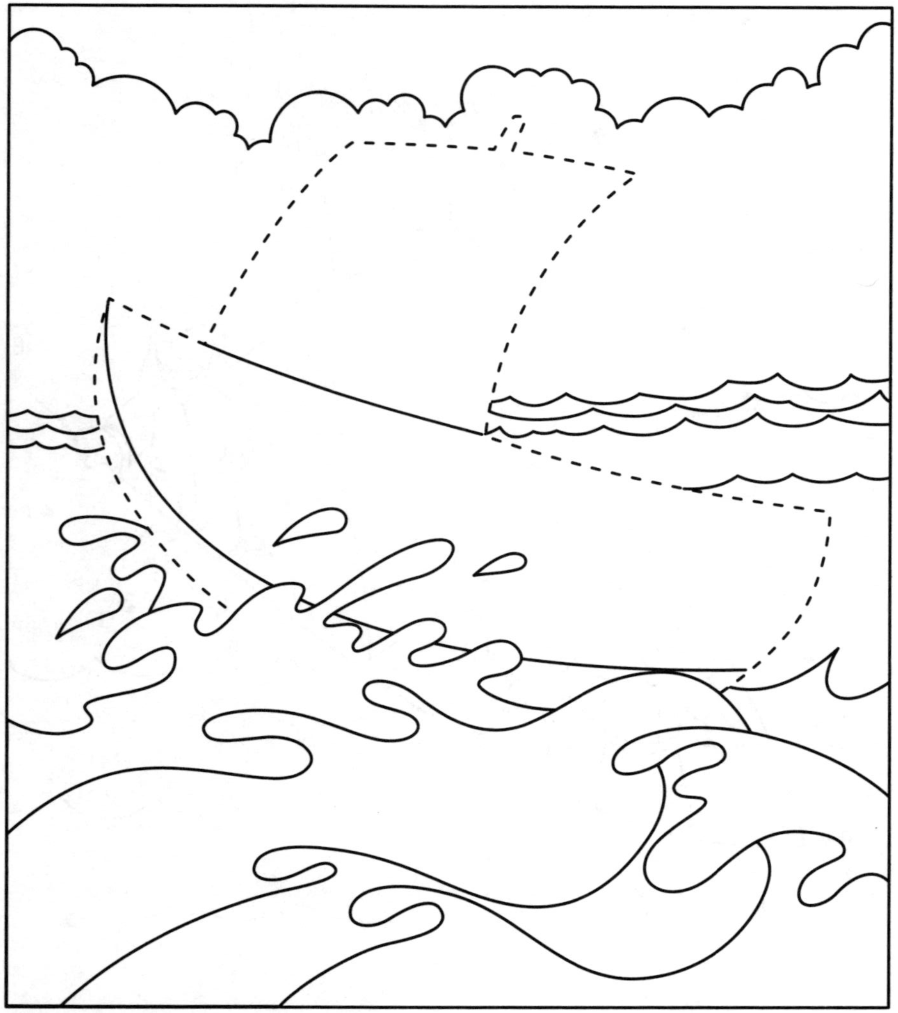

JESUS WAS SLEEPING DURING THE STORM.

The disciples woke Jesus because they were frightened. Circle the two pictures that are the same.

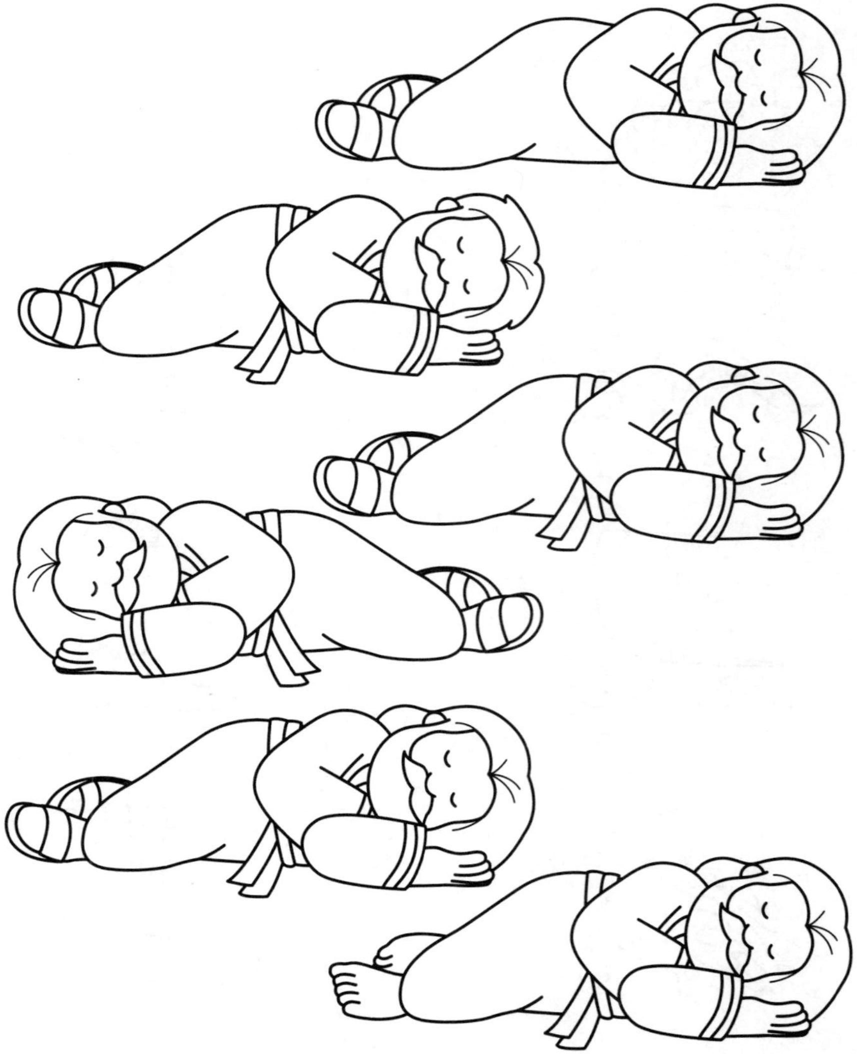

62

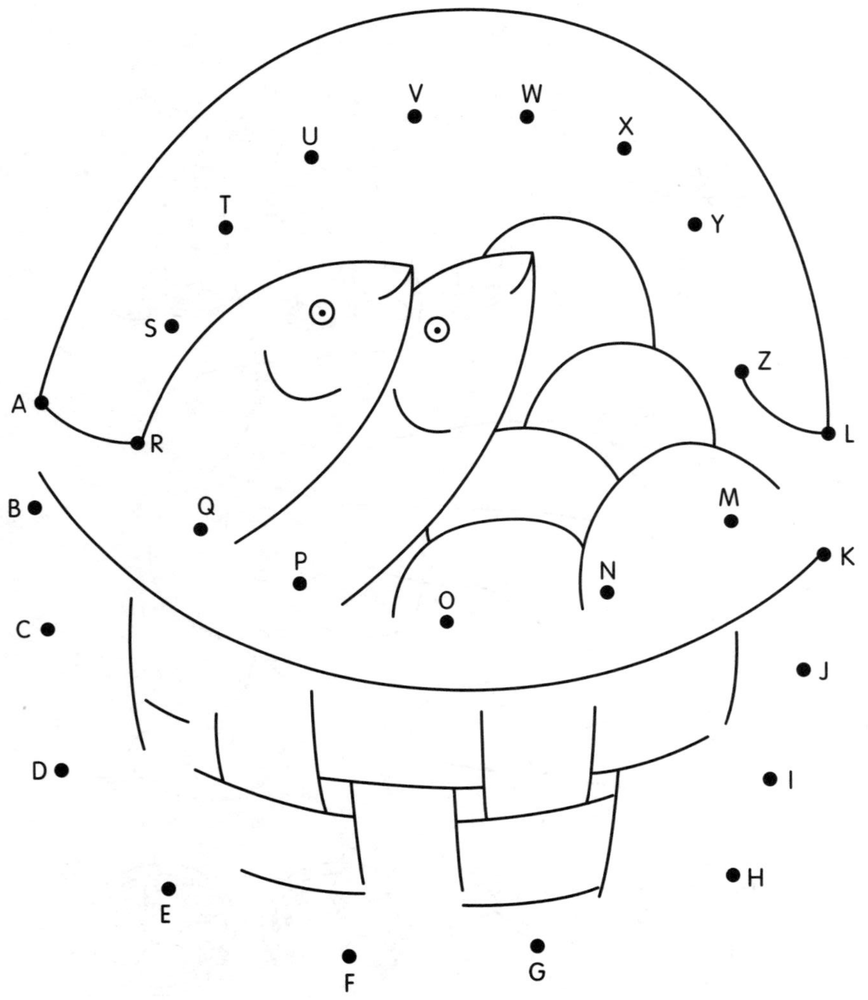

GROWING IN GRACE

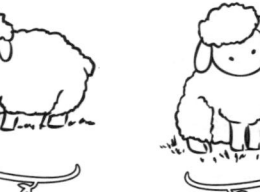

JESUS FEEDS 5,000
Matthew 14:13–21; John 6:9

A large crowd gathered to hear Jesus speak. Find and circle the objects hidden in the picture.

THE PEOPLE ATE UNTIL THEY WERE FULL.

Jesus fed the crowd with five loaves of bread and two fish. Connect the dots A–Z.

JESUS TAUGHT ABOUT THE KINGDOM OF GOD.

Jesus spoke to the crowd and healed the sick. Find and circle four things in the second picture that are different from the first picture.

A BOY HAD A BASKET WITH BREAD AND FISH.

Jesus fed the crowd with what the boy had in his basket. Follow the line from each boy. Then, circle the boy who has the basket with two fish and five loaves of bread.

64

GROWING IN GRACE

THE MIRACLES OF JESUS
Matthew 14:22–26

Jesus walked on water. Find and circle the objects hidden in the picture.

JESUS HEALED PETER'S MOTHER-IN-LAW.
Matthew 8:14–15

Jesus touched the woman's hand and the fever left her. Connect the dots 0–26.

Growing in Grace Children's Bulletins • CD-204028

© Carson-Dellosa

JESUS BROUGHT LAZARUS BACK TO LIFE.
John 11:43-44

Follow the line from each picture. Then, circle which Jesus brought Lazarus back to life.

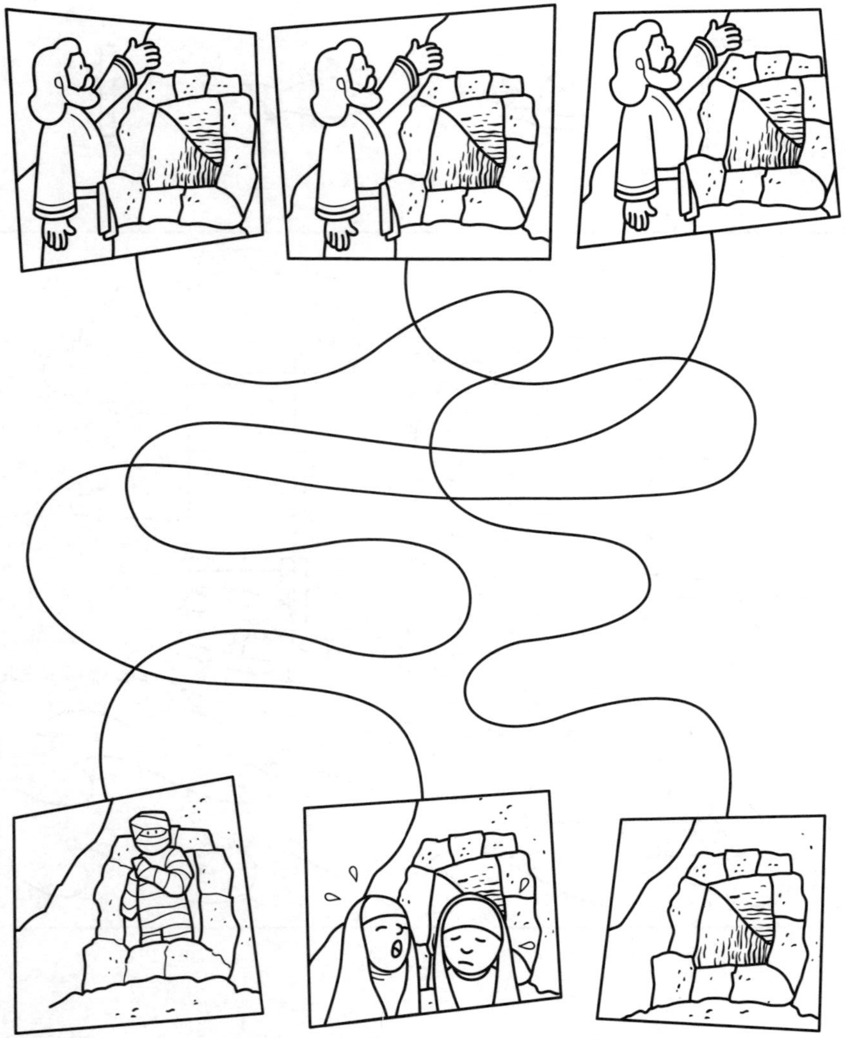

JESUS TOUCHED THE MAN AND SAID, "I AM WILLING."
Luke 5:12-13

Jesus healed a leper. Write each letter in order on the lines below as you follow the path.

66

GROWING IN GRACE

THE GOOD SAMARITAN
Luke 10:25–27

Jesus taught us to love God and our neighbor. Trace the dotted line.

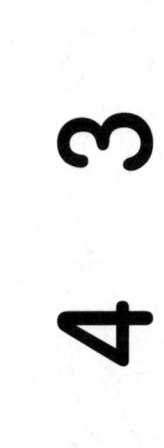

Love God with all your heart.

JESUS WANTS US TO LOVE OUR NEIGHBORS.

Count the hearts in each box and circle the correct number.

2 3 4 
3 4 5 
1 2 3 
4 3 2

Growing in Grace Children's Bulletins • CD-204028

© Carson-Dellosa

A MAN WAS HURT BY ROBBERS AS HE WALKED ALONG A ROAD.

A priest and a Levite passed by the man. Connect the dots A–Z.

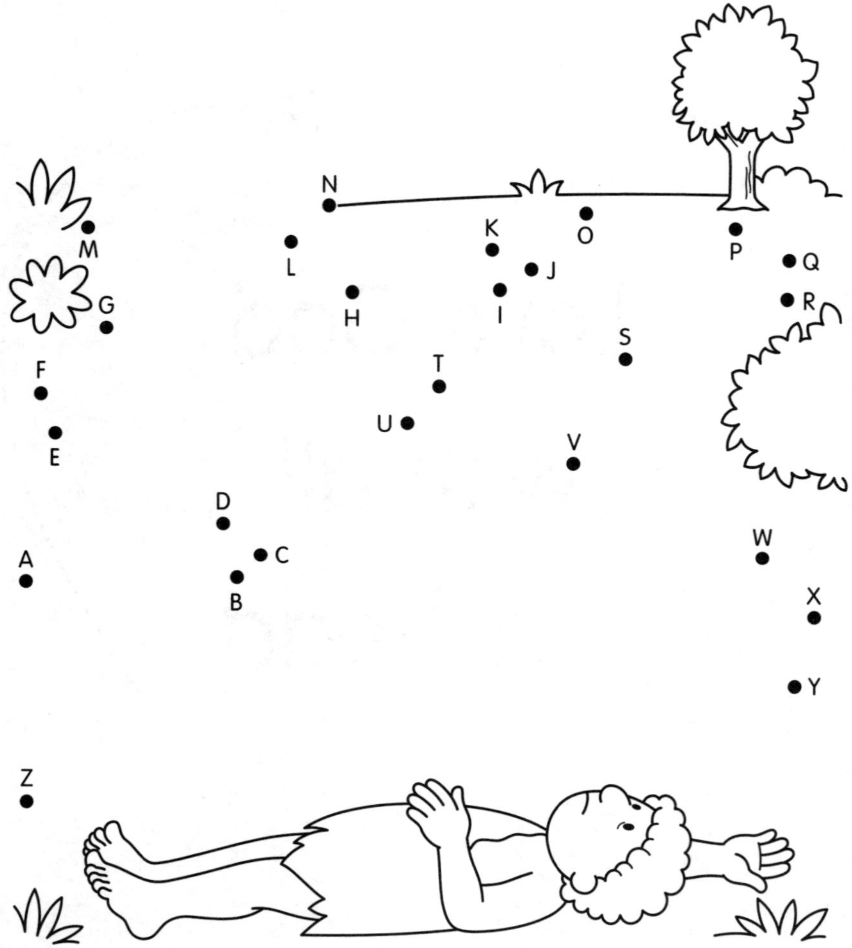

A SAMARITAN SAW THE HURT MAN AND HELPED HIM.

A Samaritan took pity on the hurt man. Find and circle the priest and the Levite hidden in the picture below.

GROWING IN GRACE

THE LOST SHEEP
Matthew 18:10–14

The shepherd left 99 sheep to find the one that was missing. Help the shepherd find his lost sheep.

Start

Finish

THE SHEPHERD WAS HAPPY TO FIND THE LOST SHEEP.

The shepherd was happier about finding one lost sheep than about the 99 sheep that did not wander off. Connect the dots 0–20.

© Carson-Dellosa

Growing in Grace Children's Bulletins • CD-204028

THE SHEPHERD SEARCHED FOR THE LOST SHEEP.

The shepherd left his flock and searched for the one sheep that wandered off. Find and circle the sheep hidden in the picture below.

THE SHEPHERD LOVED ALL OF HIS SHEEP.

The shepherd did not want any of his sheep to get lost. Circle the one sheep that is different from the others.

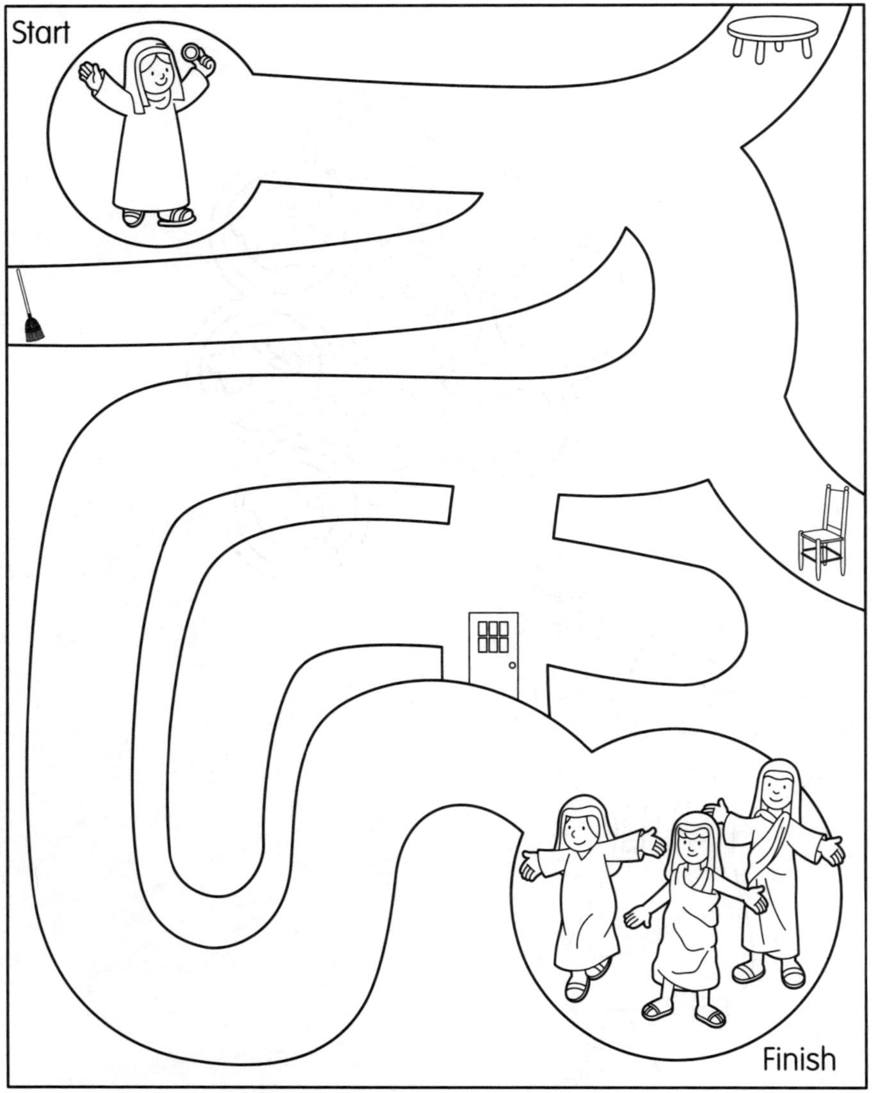

GROWING IN GRACE

THE PARABLE OF THE LOST COIN
Luke 15:8–10

A woman had 10 coins and lost one. Find and circle the coin hidden in the picture.

SHE CELEBRATED WITH HER FRIENDS.

Help the woman find her friends.

© Carson-Dellosa

Growing in Grace Children's Bulletins • CD-204028

THE WOMAN LOOKED EVERYWHERE.

Count the coins in each box and circle the correct number.

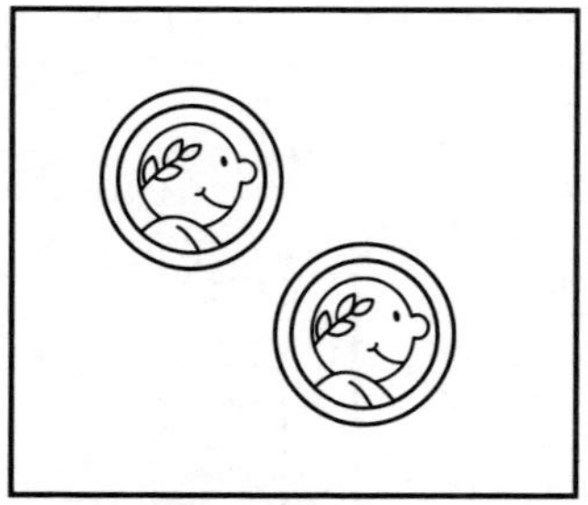

1 2 3

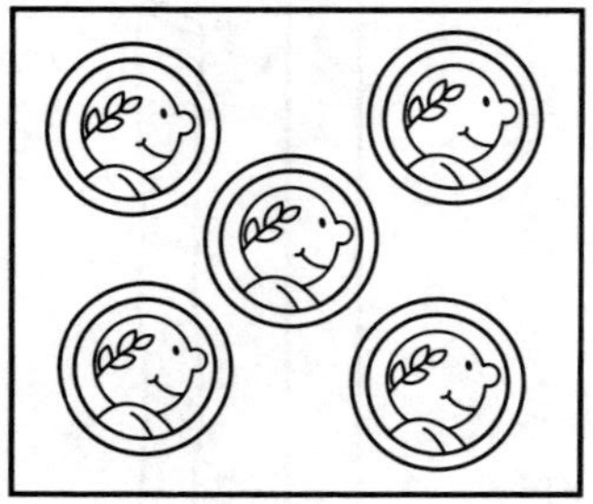

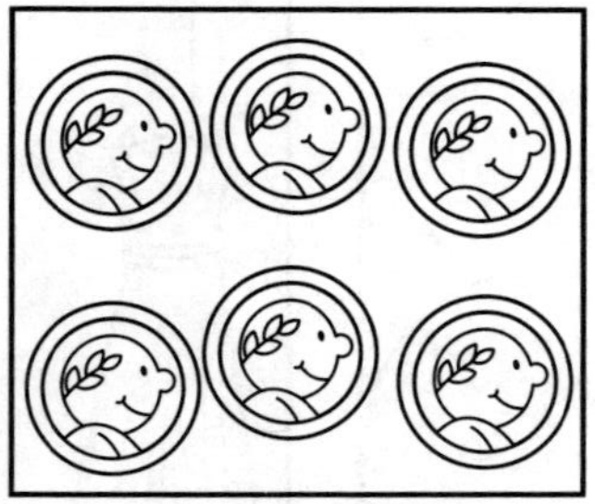

4 5 6

5 6 7

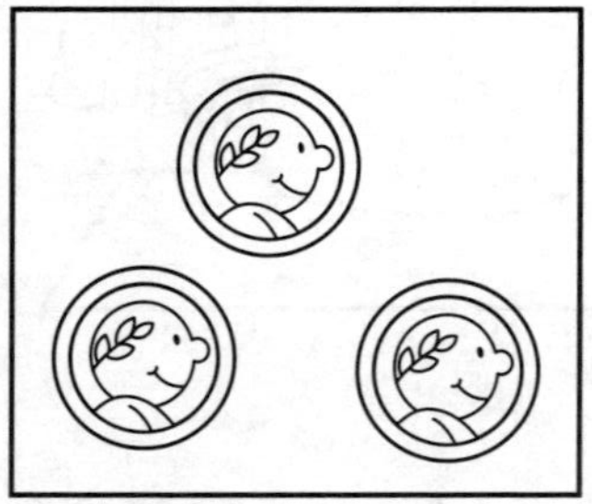

3 2 1

THE WOMAN FOUND HER COIN!

When the woman found her coin, she said, "Rejoice with me!" Find and circle one coin in the group that is different from the others.

GROWING IN GRACE

LET THE CHILDREN COME TO ME
Matthew 19:14–15, 18:1–6 NLT

Jesus blessed the children. Find the objects hidden in the picture.

JESUS LOVES LITTLE CHILDREN.

Jesus loves you! Draw a picture of yourself in the frame below.

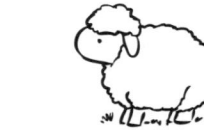

© Carson-Dellosa

Growing in Grace Children's Bulletins • CD-204028

WHOEVER WELCOMES A CHILD, WELCOMES ME.

Match the numbers with the letters. Then, write the letters on the lines to find out what belongs to those who become like children.

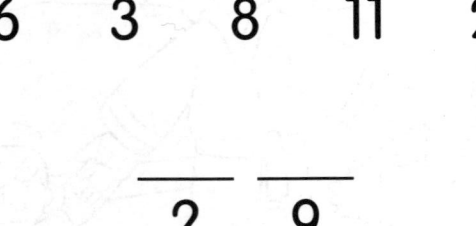

A	D	E	F	G	H	I	K	M	N	O	V
12	11	10	9	8	7	6	5	4	3	2	1

__ __ __ __ __ __   __ __
5 6 3 8 11 2   9 2

__ __ __ __ __ __ __
7 10 12 1 10 3

JESUS BLESSES THE CHILDREN.

Jesus blesses you, too! Connect the dots A–Z.

GROWING IN GRACE

UP A TREE
Luke 19:1-9

Zacchaeus wanted to see Jesus, so he climbed a tree to see over the crowds. Connect the dots A–L.

JESUS VISITED ZACCHAEUS.

Jesus told Zacchaeus that He had to stay at his house. Circle five things that are wrong in this picture.

© Carson-Dellosa

Growing in Grace Children's Bulletins • CD-204028

JESUS SAW ZACCHAEUS IN A TREE.

Trace the letters to find out what Jesus said to Zacchaeus.

Jesus said, "COME DOWN!"

ZACCHAEUS CAME DOWN FROM THE TREE.

Help Zacchaeus get down from the tree.

Start

Finish

GROWING IN GRACE

JESUS IS KING!
Matthew 21:1–11; John 12:13

Jesus rode into Jerusalem. Help Jesus ride through the city.

THE CROWDS SHOUTED, "HOSANNA!"

Hosanna means "Hurrah for Jesus!" Find and color the letters in the word HOSANNA hidden in the picture.

© Carson-Dellosa

Growing in Grace Children's Bulletins • CD-204028

JESUS RODE A DONKEY INTO JERUSALEM.

As Jesus came near the city, the crowd began to praise God. Count and circle the number of pictures.

3   4   5   6

PEOPLE WAVED PALM BRANCHES IN PRAISE.

Trace the dotted line to complete the palm branch.

7

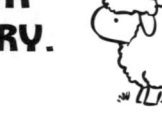

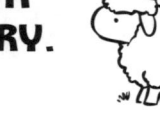

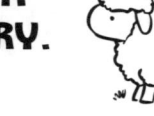

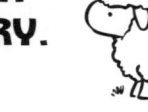

GROWING IN GRACE

JESUS WILL RETURN
Luke 21:25–36

There will be signs in the sun, moon, and stars when Jesus returns. Draw a line to connect each pair of matching shapes.

JESUS WILL COME WITH POWER AND GREAT GLORY.

Luke 21:27 says that the Son of Man will come in a cloud with power and great glory. Connect the dots 1–25.

© Carson-Dellosa

Growing in Grace Children's Bulletins • CD-204028

EVERYONE WILL SEE JESUS COMING IN A CLOUD.

Circle the two clouds that are the same.

JESUS TELLS US TO BE READY FOR HIS RETURN.

Match the letters with the pictures. Then, write the letters on the lines below to complete the verse

☺ ✝ ☆ ◎ △ ◇ ♡ ✗ # % ▢
Y W R A P T H C D N

"Be always on the

✝ ◎ ♡ # ✗ __'__

✝ __ __ __ __ __'

__ ▢ % __

△ ☆ __ __

△ ☆ ◎ ☺ __ __"

Luke 21:36

GROWING IN GRACE

JESUS SETS THE EXAMPLE
John 13

Jesus washed all of the disciples' feet. Help Jesus wash the disciple's feet in the picture below.

Start → Finish

JESUS TAUGHT US TO SERVE.

Draw a line to connect each picture on the left to what it is missing.

Growing in Grace Children's Bulletins • CD-204028

JESUS SHOWED THE DISCIPLES HIS LOVE.

Circle the picture that matches the first picture in each row.

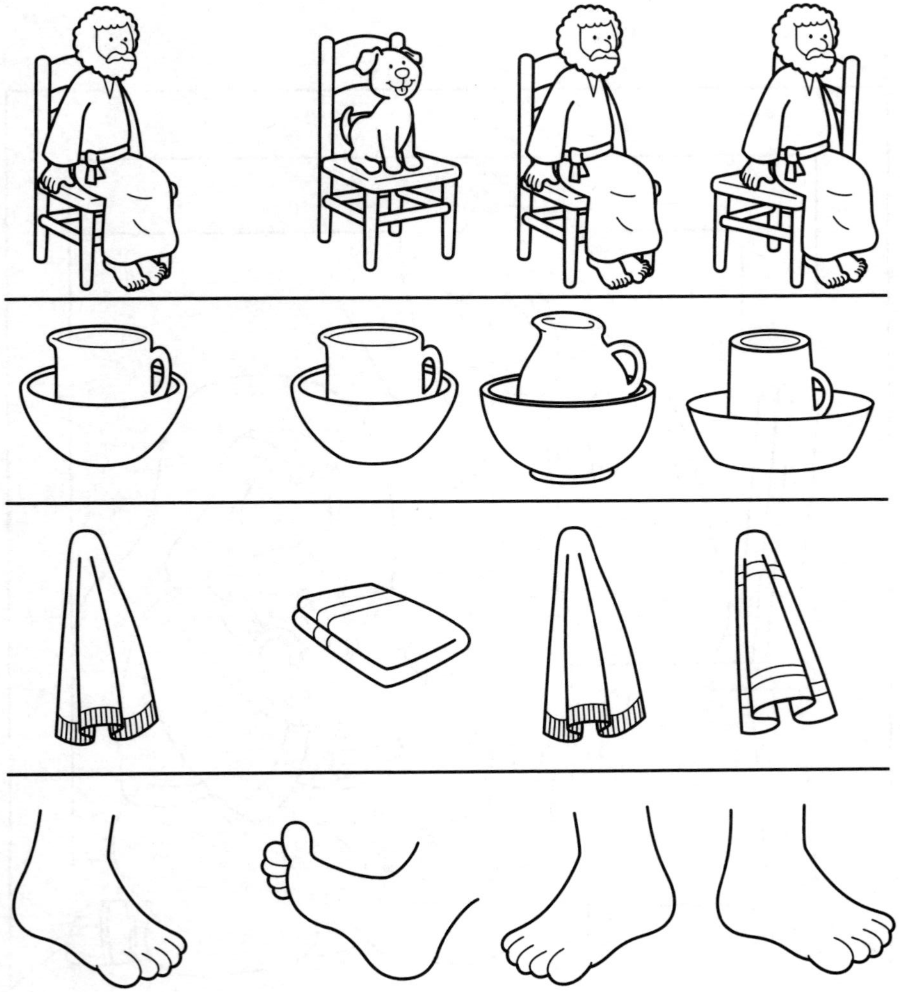

NO SERVANT IS GREATER THAN HIS MASTER.

Jesus set an example for us to be a servant to others. Follow the path from each letter to find out what Jesus wants us to do. Then, write the letters on the lines below.

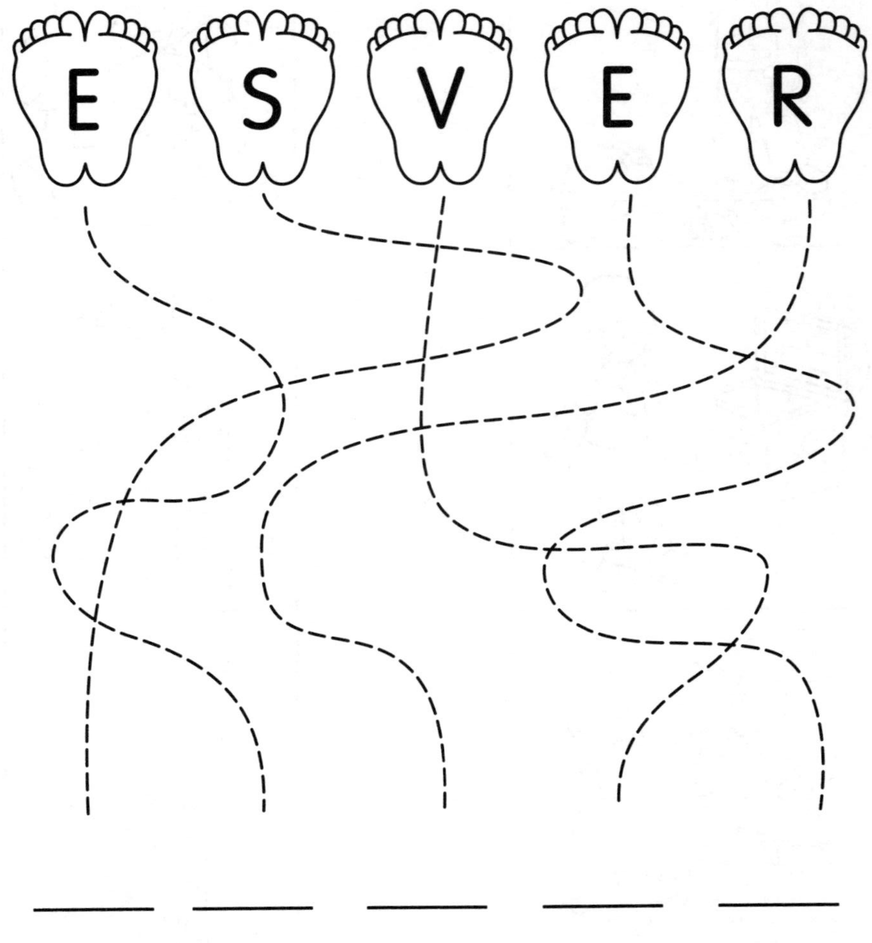

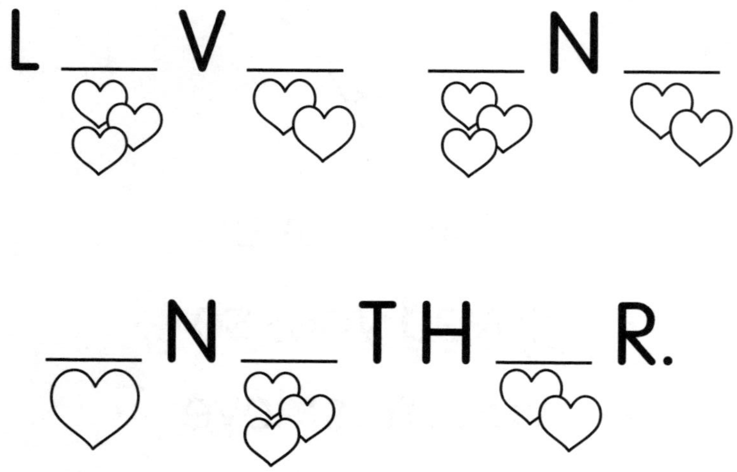

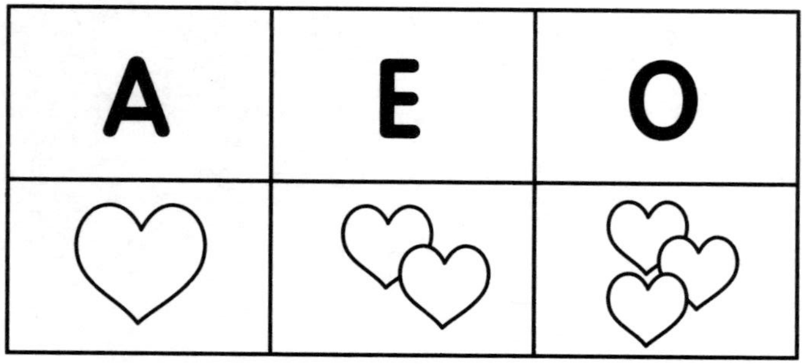

GROWING IN GRACE

A NEW COMMAND
John 13:34

Jesus gave us a new command: to love as He loves. Complete the hearts by tracing the dotted lines. Then, count and circle the number of hearts.

5   6   7   8

WHOM DOES JESUS WANT US TO LOVE?

Match the letters to the pictures. Then, write the letters on the lines to find out whom Jesus tells us to love.

L __ V __ __ N __

__ N __ TH __ R.

A	E	O

JESUS' NEW COMMAND IS ABOUT LOVE.

Jesus said that we must love one another as He loves us. Draw a line to connect each pair of matching pictures.

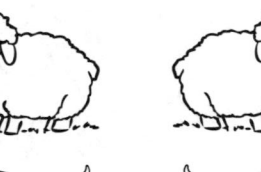

LOVE ONE ANOTHER AS I HAVE LOVED YOU.

Connect the dots 0–20.

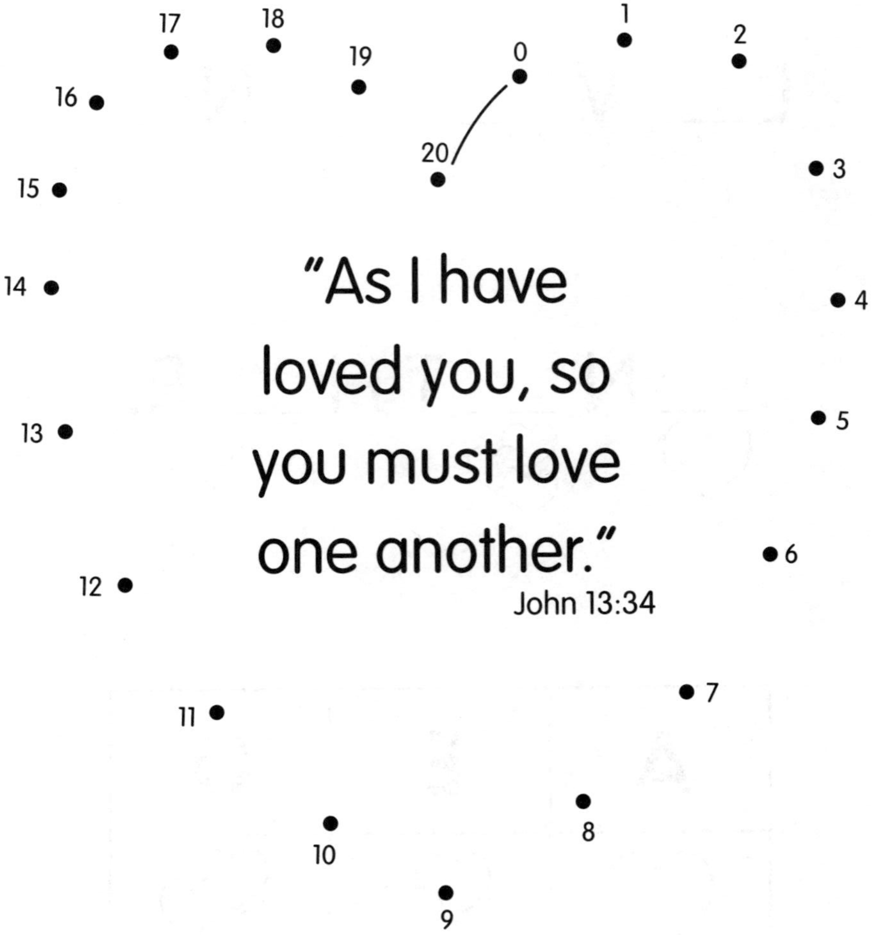

"As I have loved you, so you must love one another."

John 13:34

GROWING IN GRACE

HOLY WEEK
Luke 19:28-44; 20-23; 24:1-12

Many events took place during Jesus' last week on Earth. Draw lines to connect the pictures that belong together.

DON'T KNOW HIM.

JESUS DIED ON A CROSS FOR YOU.

Complete the cross and color it.

JESUS PRAYED IN THE GARDEN.

Circle the picture below that matches the one of Jesus praying in the garden.

JESUS SAID, "REMEMBER ME."

At the Passover meal, Jesus gave bread and wine to his disciples. Connect the dots 1–15.

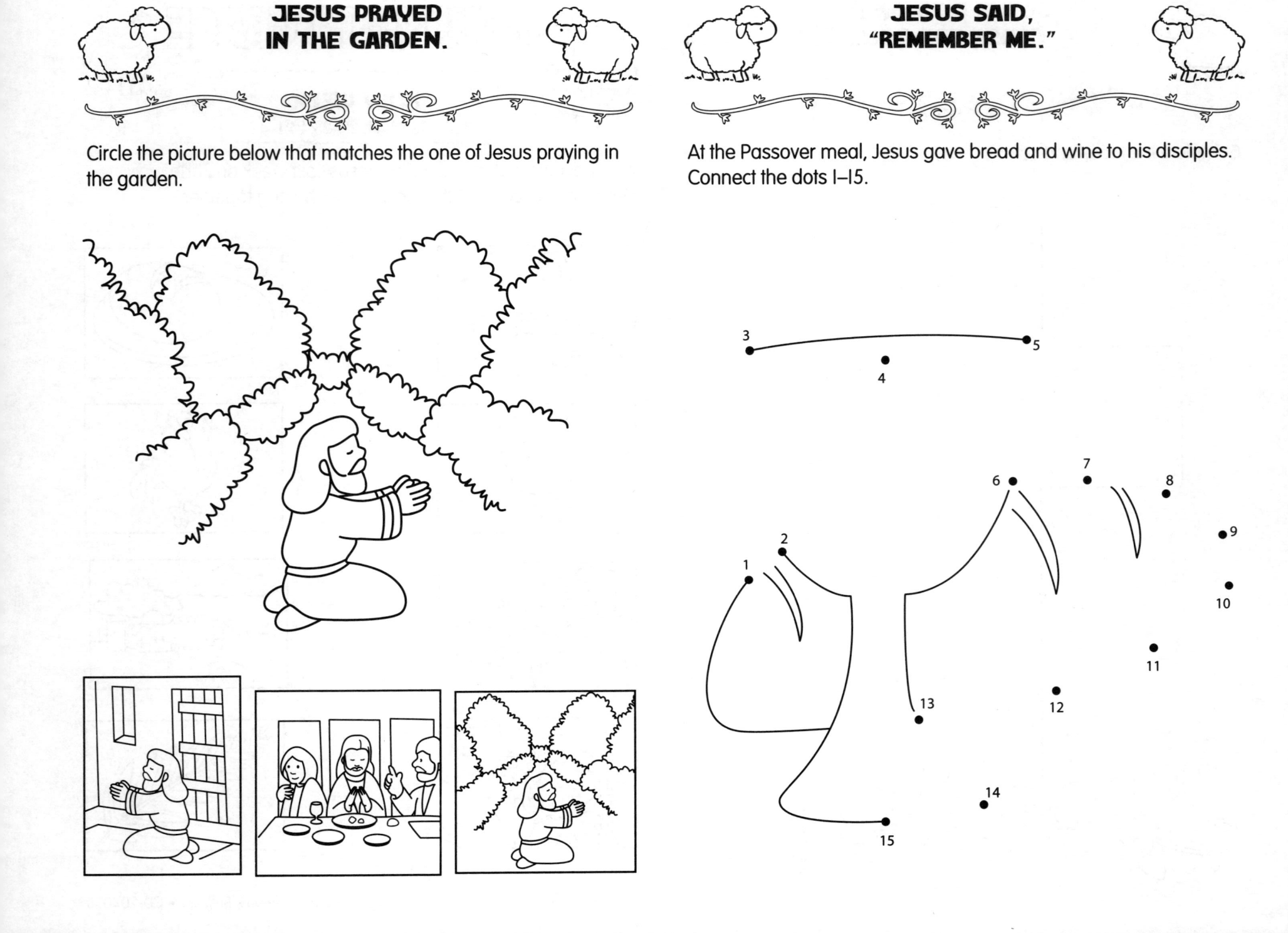

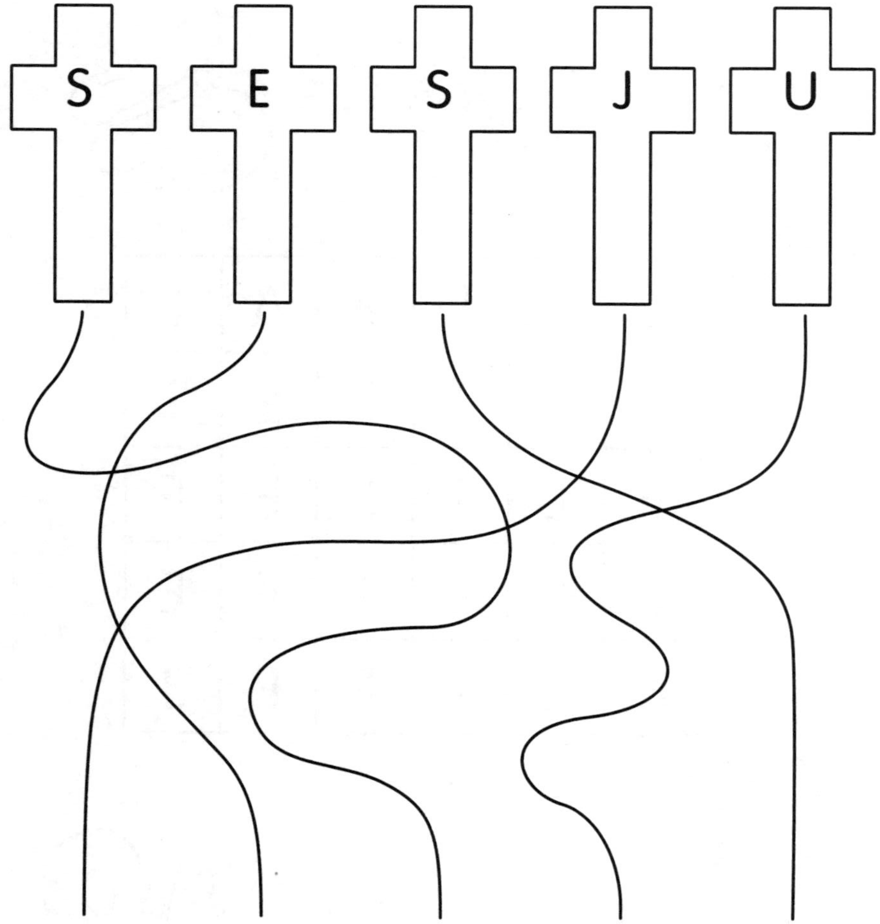

GROWING IN GRACE

THE WAY TO THE FATHER
John 14:6

Trace the letters and read what Jesus said.

Jesus said, "I am the

THE BIBLE TELLS US THE WAY TO GOD, THE FATHER.

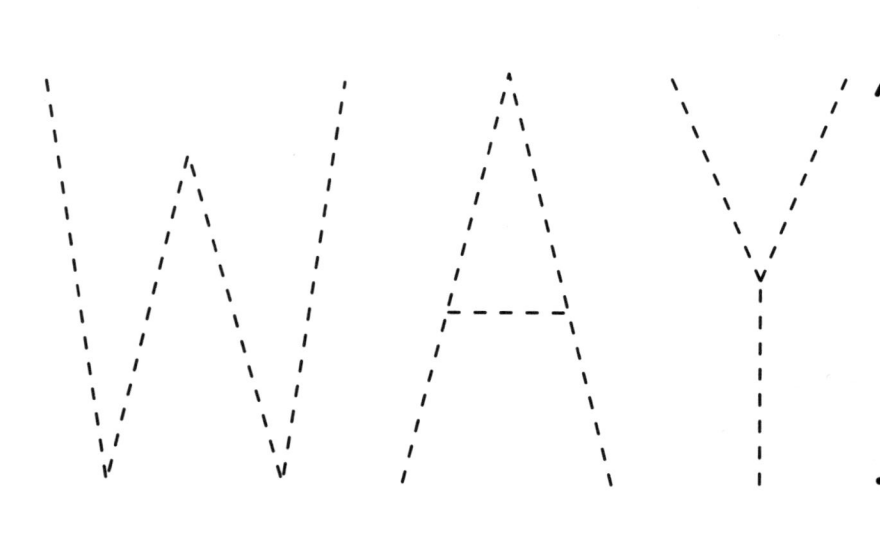

Follow the path from each letter. Then, write the letter on the line to find out the name of God's Son.

S E S J U

© Carson-Dellosa

Growing in Grace Children's Bulletins • CD-204028

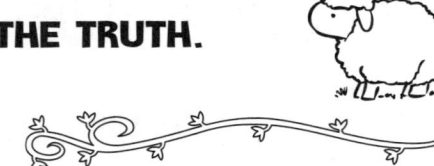

JESUS IS THE TRUTH.

Jesus told His disciples that He is the way and the life. Use the code to find out what else Jesus said.

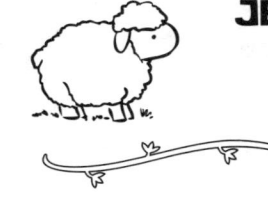

⇩	U
⇦	T
⇧	R
⇨	H

I am the

⇦ ⇧ ⇩ ⇦ ⇨ _____ !

JESUS IS THE WAY AND THE TRUTH AND THE LIFE.

Find and circle the word LIFE seven times in the puzzle below.

L	I	F	E	A	L
I	L	I	F	E	I
F	L	M	I	F	F
E	M	L	F	E	E
K	E	I	E	I	J

GROWING IN GRACE

HE IS RISEN
John 20:1–20; Matthew 28:2–3

The tomb in which Jesus was buried was empty. Connect the dots A–V.

JESUS' DEATH OFFERS LIFE TO EVERYONE.

Put the story of Jesus' death and resurrection in order by drawing lines from the pictures to the numbers.

1

2

3

4

Growing in Grace Children's Bulletins • CD-204028

© Carson-Dellosa

AN ANGEL ROLLED BACK THE STONE.

An angel came down from heaven, rolled the stone away from the tomb, and sat on it. Connect the dots A–Z.

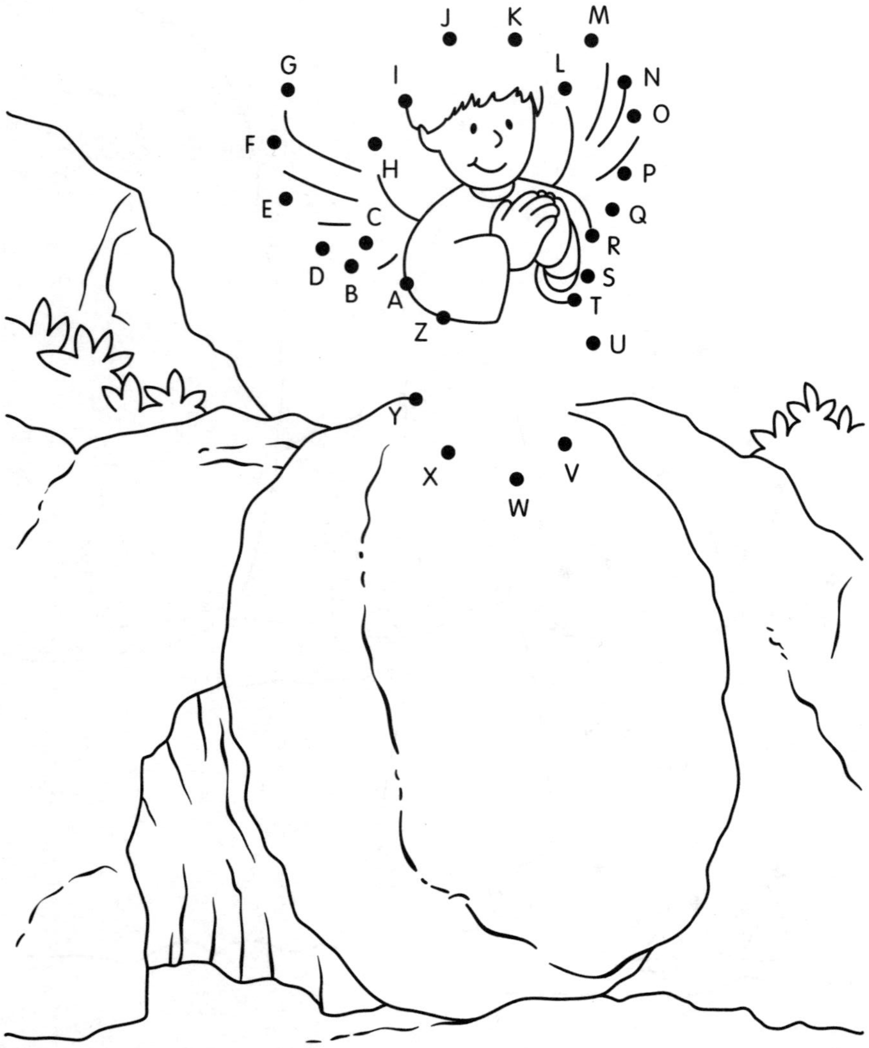

JESUS APPEARED TO MARY.

Mary Magdalene went to the tomb and saw Jesus standing there. Find the objects hidden in the picture below.

90

GROWING IN GRACE

GOD GAVE US JESUS
John 3:16

God loved the world so much that He sent us His only Son. Find and circle the word *LOVE* five times in the word search.

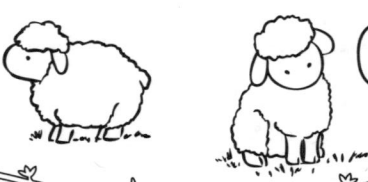

L	S	X	L	C	A
O	A	L	O	V	E
V	N	F	V	U	J
E	M	T	E	L	K
B	C	D	Y	O	P
	H	N	P	V	E
		L	O	V	E

WHOEVER BELIEVES IN JESUS HAS ETERNAL LIFE.

Draw the happy faces of the believers. Then, draw your face and hair, too!

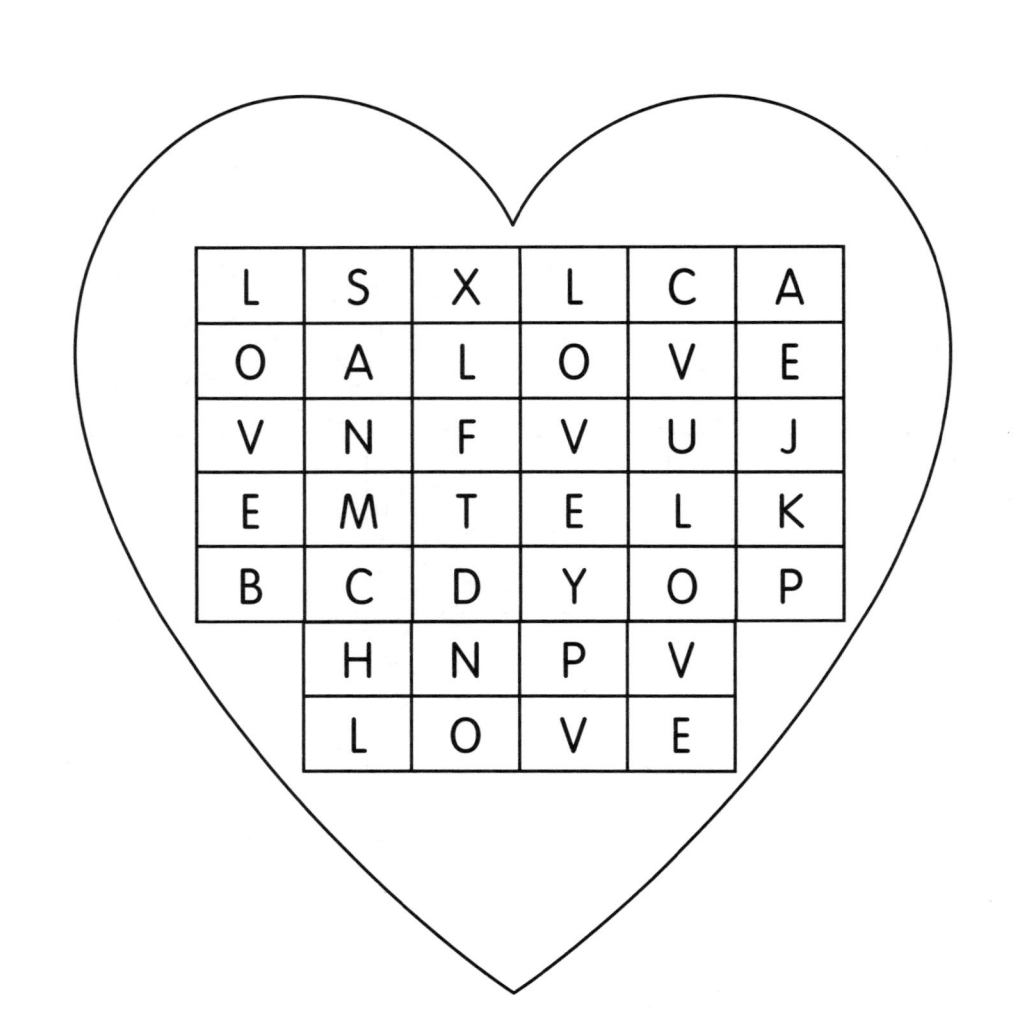

© Carson-Dellosa

Growing in Grace Children's Bulletins • CD-204028

GOD GIVES US LIFE IN HIS SON.

Color each shape that has a ♡ to find out who God's Son is.

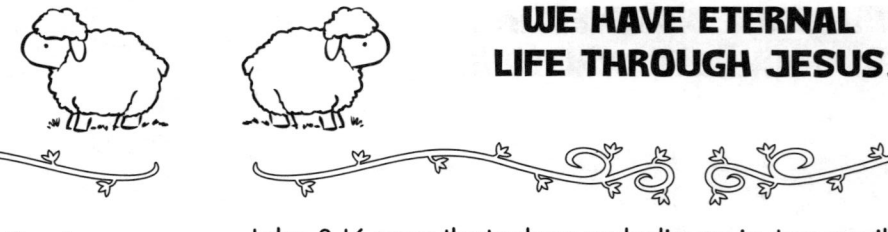

WE HAVE ETERNAL LIFE THROUGH JESUS.

John 3:16 says that whoever believes in Jesus will have eternal life. Write the letter e on each blank space below.

Hav___ lif___ t___rnal through m___.

GROWING IN GRACE

THE HOLY SPIRIT COMES
Acts 2:1–13

The Holy Spirit sounded like a blowing wind when He came from heaven and filled the house. Color the shapes with a ● orange. Then, color the shapes with a – blue.

THE PEOPLE HEARD THEIR OWN LANGUAGES SPOKEN.

Everyone in the crowd heard the wonders of God spoken in their own language. Trace the letters to find out how everyone felt.

TONGUES OF FIRE CAME TO REST ON THE DISCIPLES.

Connect the dots 0–20 to see what appeared to rest on the disciples when the Holy Spirit came.

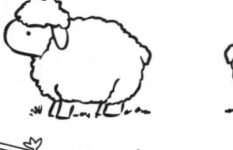

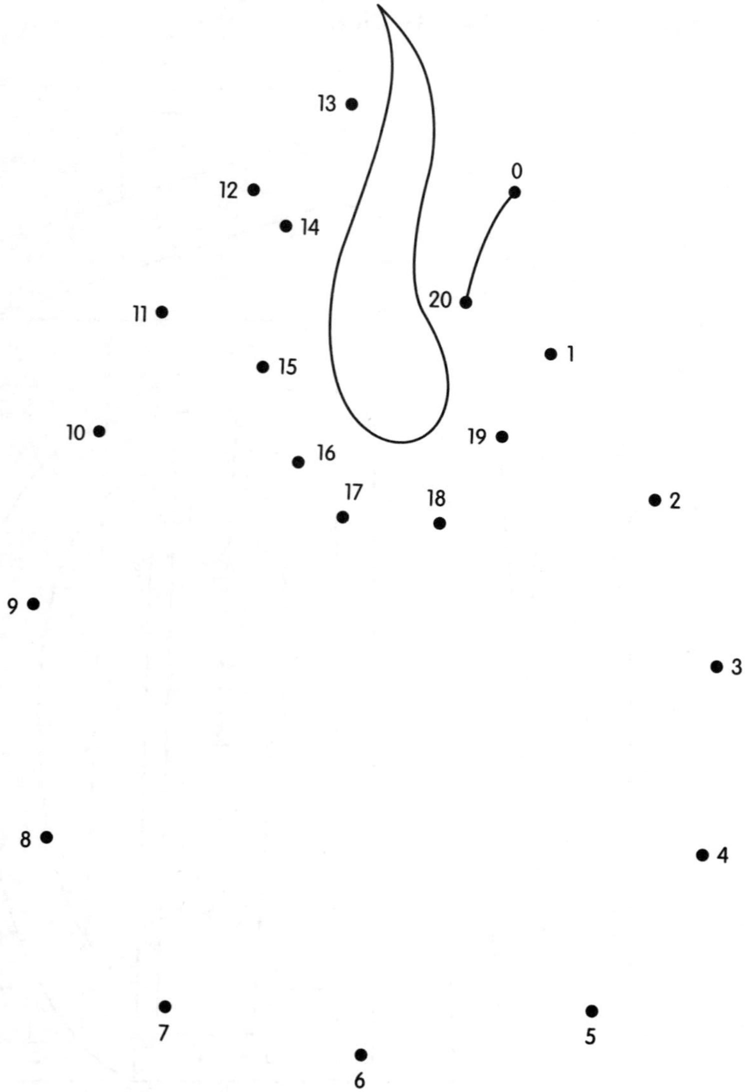

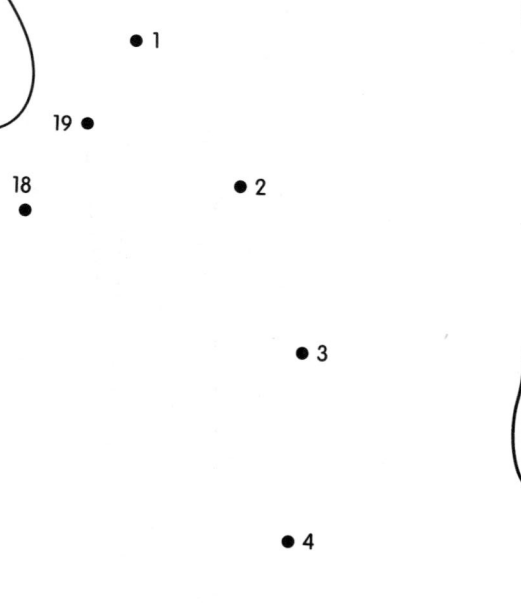

THE DISCIPLES WERE FILLED WITH THE HOLY SPIRIT.

Filled with the Spirit, the disciples began to speak in other tongues. Find and color the two disciples who match.

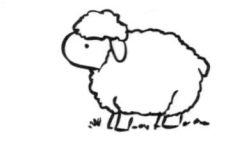

GROWING IN GRACE

SAUL SEES THE LIGHT
Acts 9:1–22 NLT

Saul was angry at anyone who followed Jesus. One day, Jesus spoke to him from a bright light. Connect the dots 1–27.

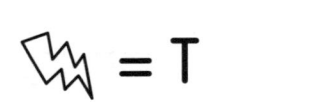

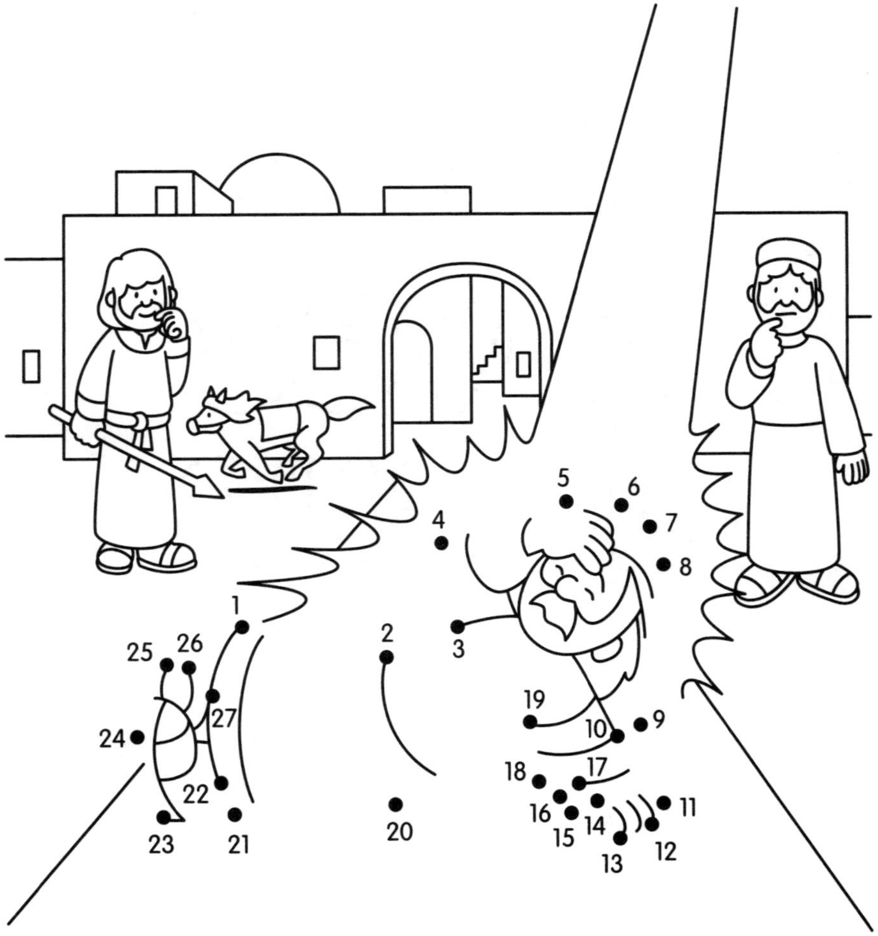

SAUL BEGAN PREACHING ABOUT JESUS.

Match the letters with the pictures. Then, write the letters on the lines to see who Saul told the people Jesus was.

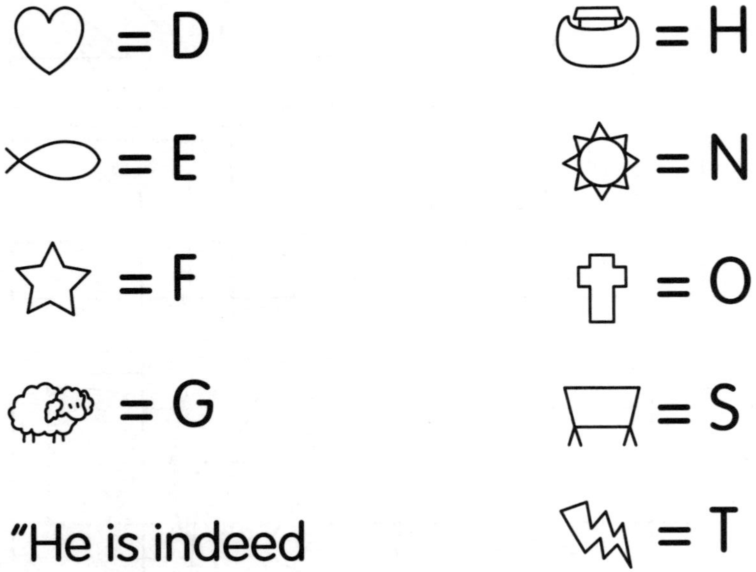

♡ = D
🐟 = E
☆ = F
🐑 = G
👜 = H
☀ = N
✝ = O
⛺ = S
⚡ = T

"He is indeed ___ ___ ___ ___ ___ ___ ___ ___ ___ !"

Acts 9:20 NLT

SAUL'S HEART WAS CHANGED.

When Saul could not see, God changed his heart. Trace the dotted line to draw the heart.

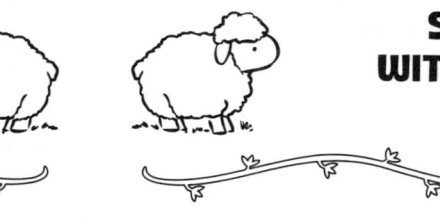

Saul loves Jesus

SAUL WAS FILLED WITH THE HOLY SPIRIT.

Saul was filled with the Holy Spirit and could see again. Find and color the hidden letters of the words *Holy Spirit*.

96

GROWING IN GRACE

FORGIVENESS
Acts 13:38

Match the pictures and letters. Then, write the letters on the lines to see the message of what you are through faith in Jesus.

A E F G I M N O R V

IN THE LORD, WE ARE FORGIVEN.

Where do you find forgiveness? Trace the letters to find out.

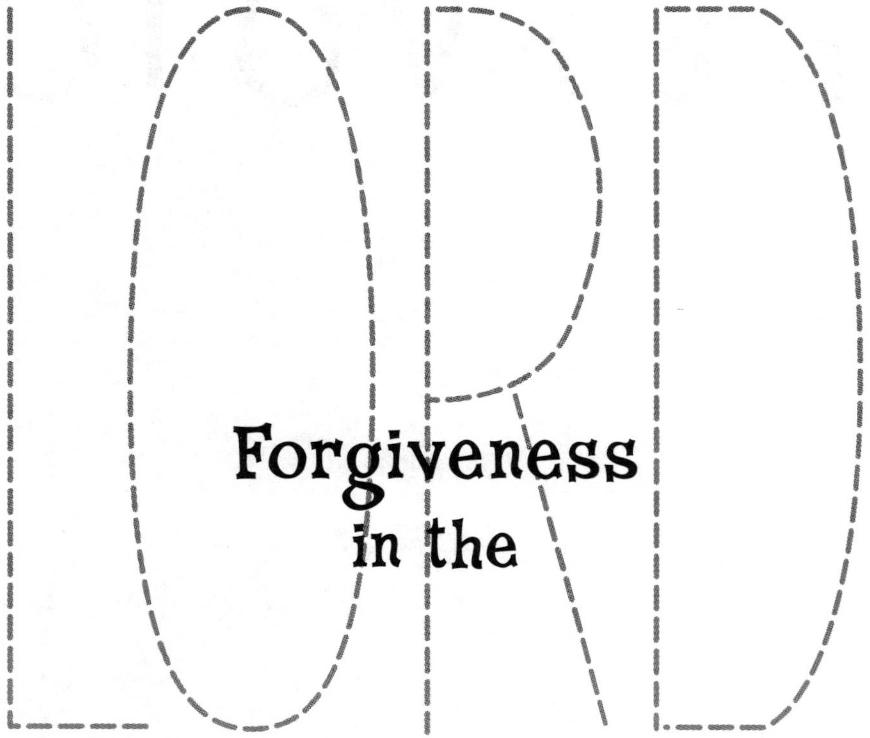

Forgiveness in the

"In him we have . . . the forgiveness of sins. . . ."
Ephesians 1:7

© Carson-Dellosa   Growing in Grace Children's Bulletins • CD-204028

JESUS SAID TO NEVER STOP FORGIVING.

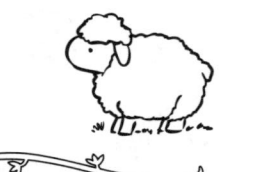

According to Matthew 18:22 NLT, how many times did Jesus tell us that we should forgive? To find out, color the two boxes that are the same.

70 × 7

50 × 7

70 × 7

1 × 7

20 × 7

55 × 7

FORGIVE AS GOD FORGIVES YOU.

Ephesians 4:32 tells us what we must do as Christ did. Follow the path from each letter. Then, write the letter on each line below to find out what we must do.

R E F V O I G

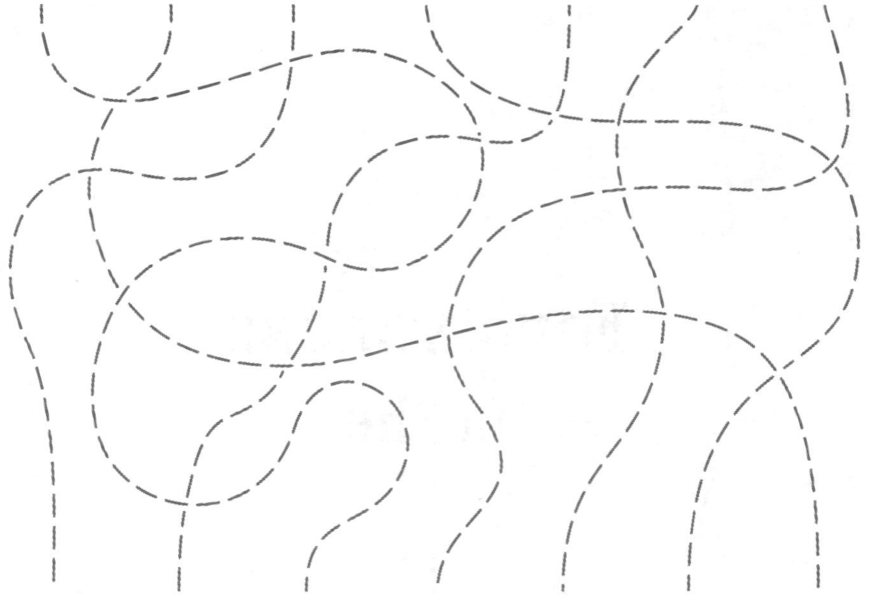

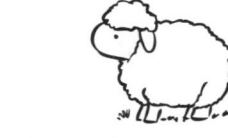

GROWING IN GRACE

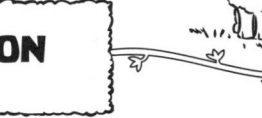

A NEW CREATION
2 Corinthians 5:17

You are a new creation in Christ! Connect the dots A–Z.

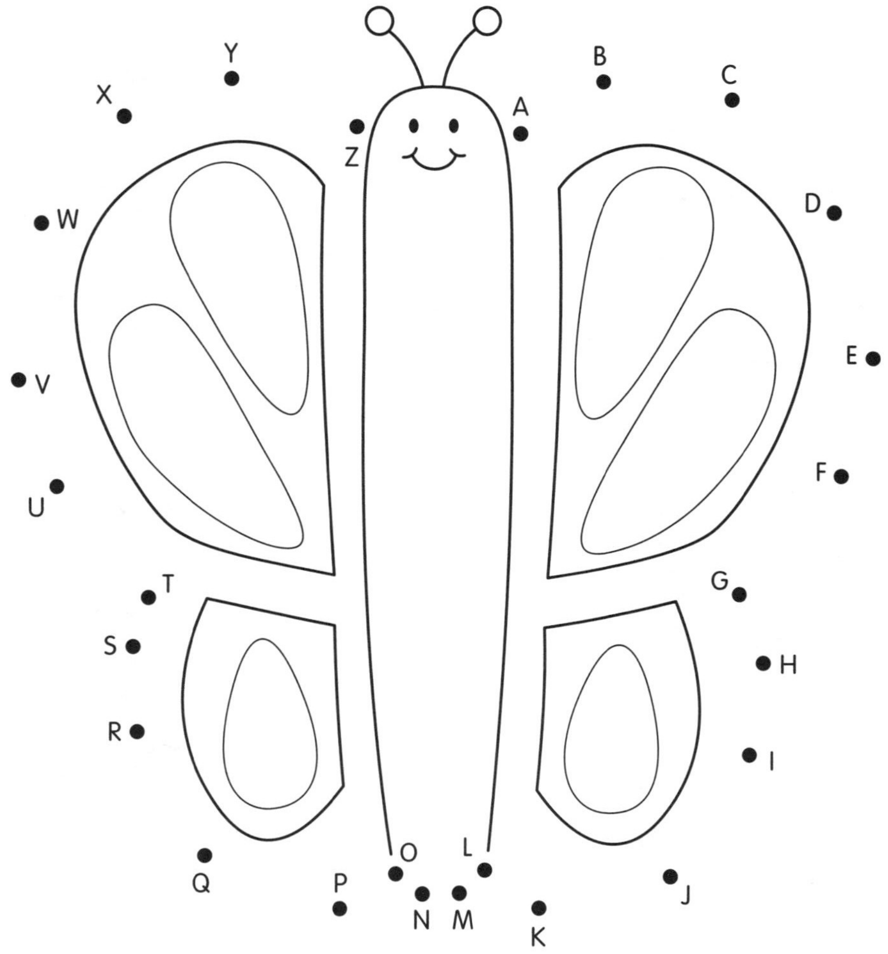

BE NEW IN CHRIST!

The old is gone and the new has come. Use the code key to see what you are now in Christ.

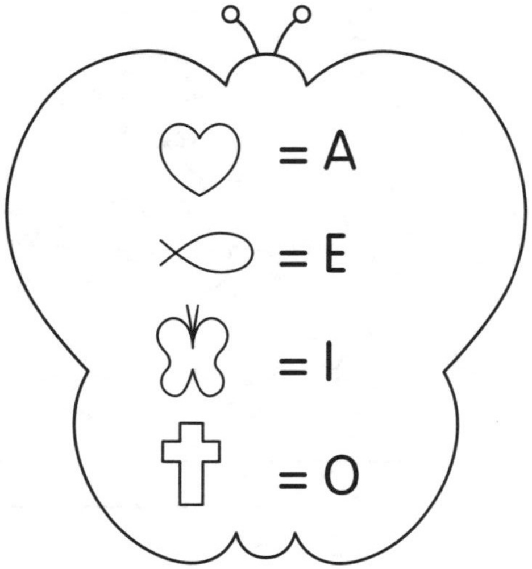

♥ = A
🐟 = E
🦋 = I
✝ = O

YOU ARE
N __ W
  ♥
C R __ __ T __ __ N!
   🐟 🦋 ✝ ♥

OUR HEARTS ARE NEW IN JESUS.

Draw a line to connect the matching hearts.

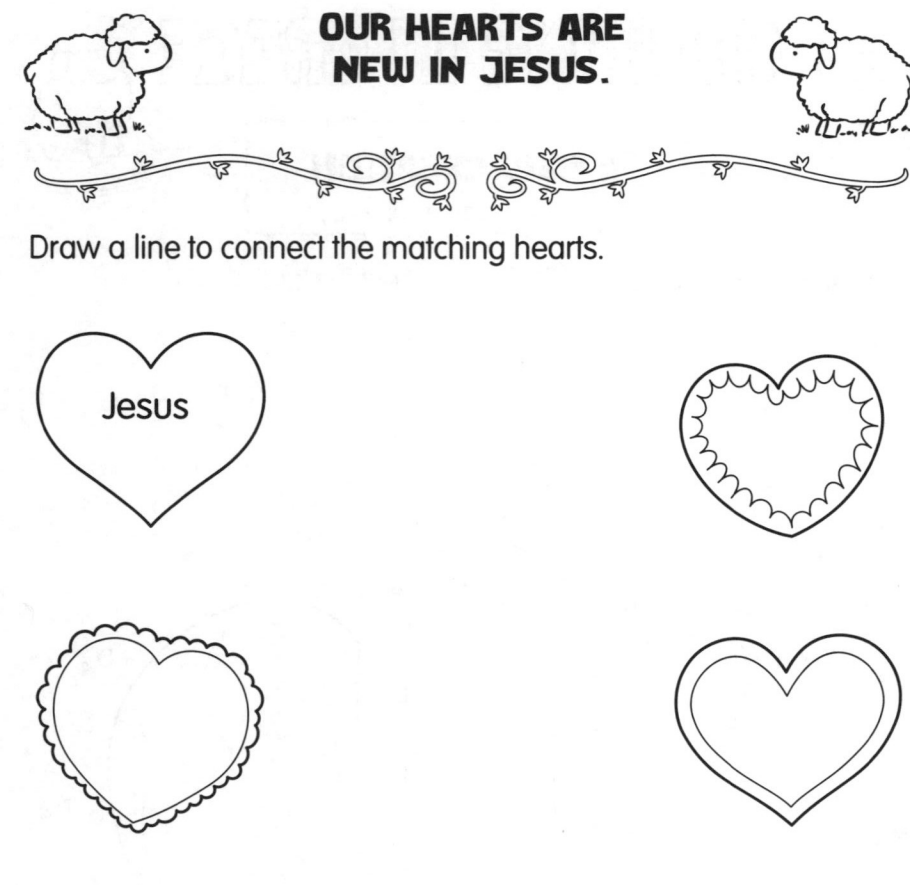

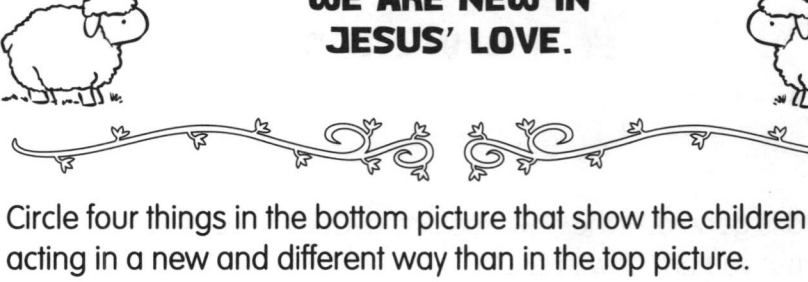

Jesus

Jesus

WE ARE NEW IN JESUS' LOVE.

Circle four things in the bottom picture that show the children acting in a new and different way than in the top picture.

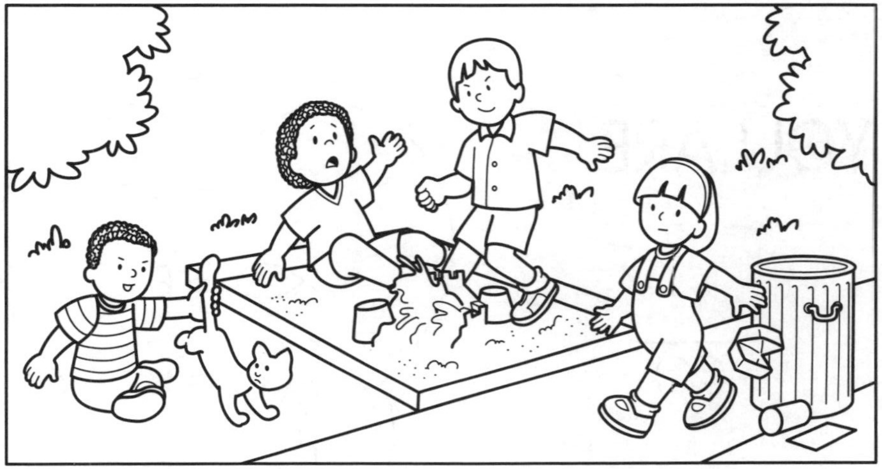

GROWING IN GRACE

SAVED BY FAITH
Ephesians 2:8-9

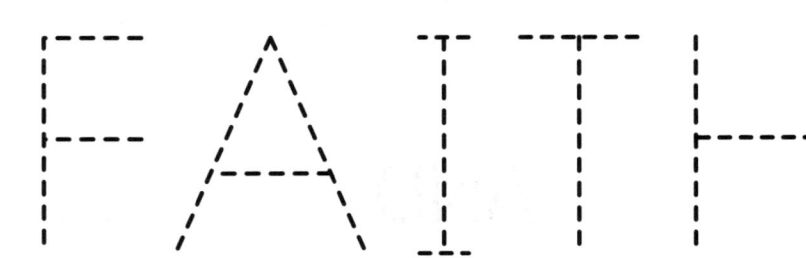

The Bible tells us that our faith in Jesus saves us. Trace each letter. Then, write each letter on a line below.

F A I T H

___ ___ ___ ___ ___

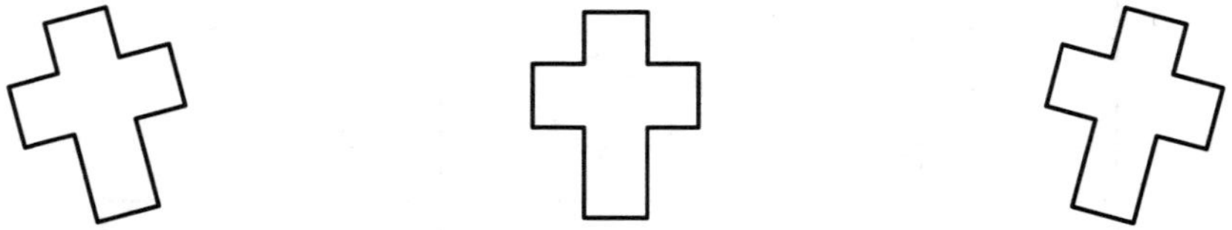

YOU ARE SAVED THROUGH FAITH.

Draw a line to connect each matching letter.

F
A
I
T
H

A
T
H
F
I

© Carson-Dellosa

Growing in Grace Children's Bulletins • CD-204028

HAVE FAITH AND BELIEVE IN JESUS.

Match the letters to the pictures. Then, write the letters on the lines to complete the words and find out what Jesus wants us to do.

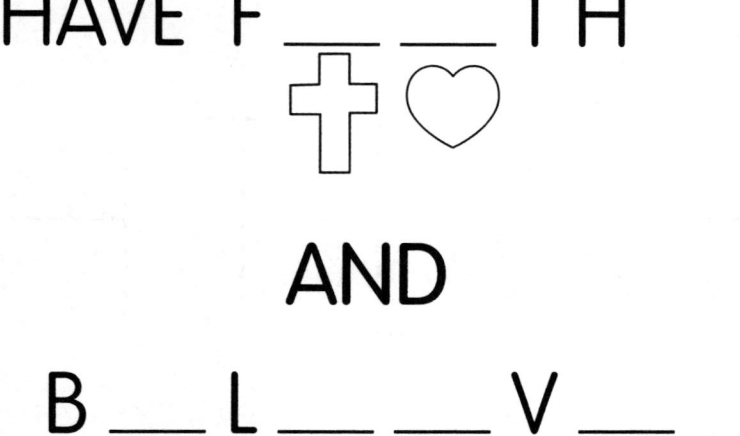

HAVE F __ __ TH

B __ L __ __ V __

AND

IN HIM.

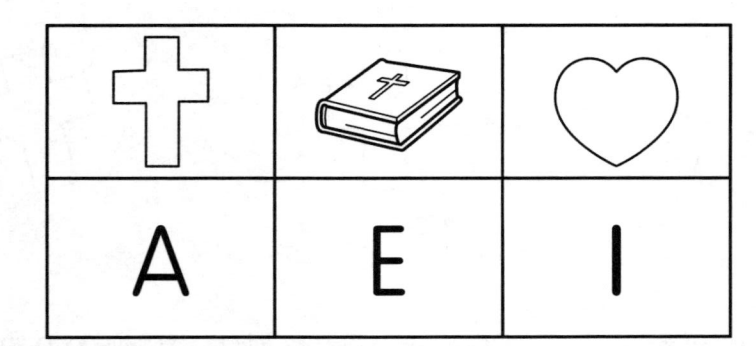

✝	📖	♡
A	E	I

BELIEVE IN JESUS, AND YOU WILL HAVE ETERNAL LIFE.

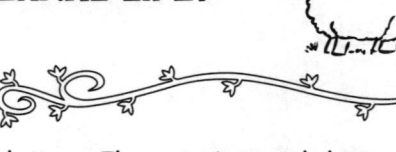

Trace the dotted line to connect the letters. Then, write each letter in order on the lines below.

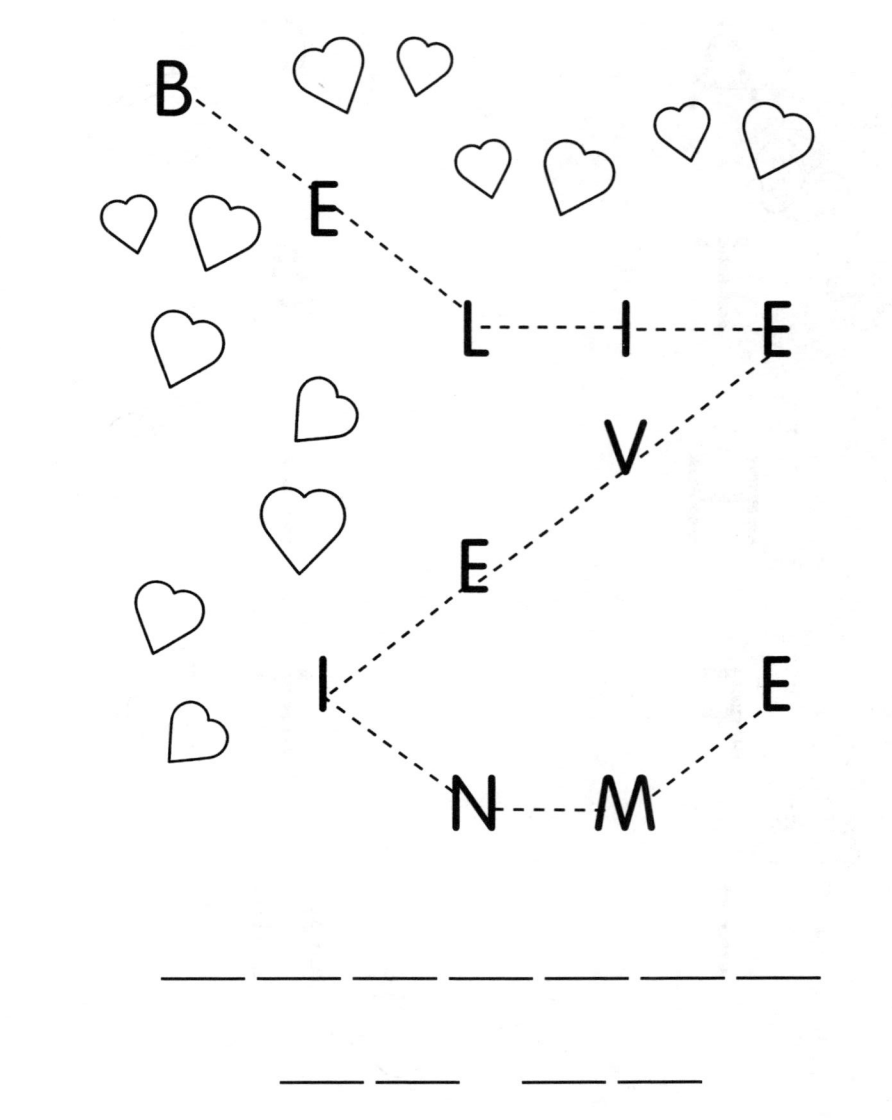

B E L I E V E
I
E
N
M
E

___ ___ ___ ___ ___ ___ ___

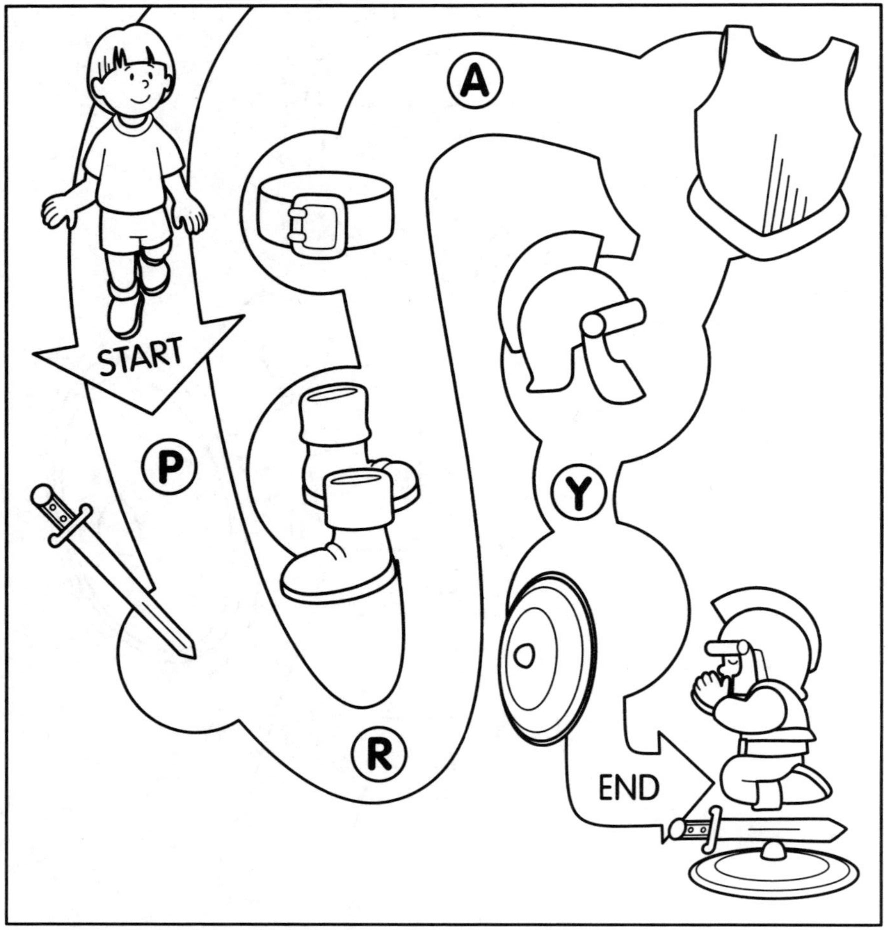

GROWING IN GRACE

ARMOR OF GOD
Ephesians 6:10–20

Match each person to his piece of missing armor.

PRAY IN THE SPIRIT ON ALL OCCASIONS.

Follow the path and write the letters in order on the lines below.

_____

TAKE UP THE SHIELD OF FAITH.

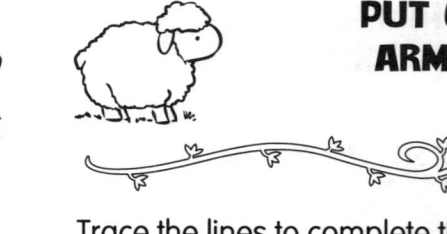

Trace the letters to write the word FAITH.

PUT ON THE FULL ARMOR OF GOD.

Trace the lines to complete the armor.

GROWING IN GRACE

GIVE THANKS
Colossians 3:16

Give thanks with a grateful heart. Follow the hearts and write the letters in order on the lines below.

Start: G H R A T E
L U F
E A R T
Finish

_____ _____

GIVE THANKS IN ALL THINGS.
1 Thessalonians 5:18

Give God thanks in all circumstances. Draw lines to connect the matching pictures.

Growing in Grace Children's Bulletins • CD-204028
© Carson-Dellosa

GIVE THANKS TO GOD FOREVER.

How long should we give God thanks? Match the letters with the pictures. Then, write the letters on the lines below to spell out the answer.

E 🕐
F ✚
O ♡
R 📖
V ✋

___ ___ ___ ___ ___
✚   ♡   📖 ✋   🕐

PRAISE GOD WITH MUSIC.

Connect the dots A–T to complete the picture below.

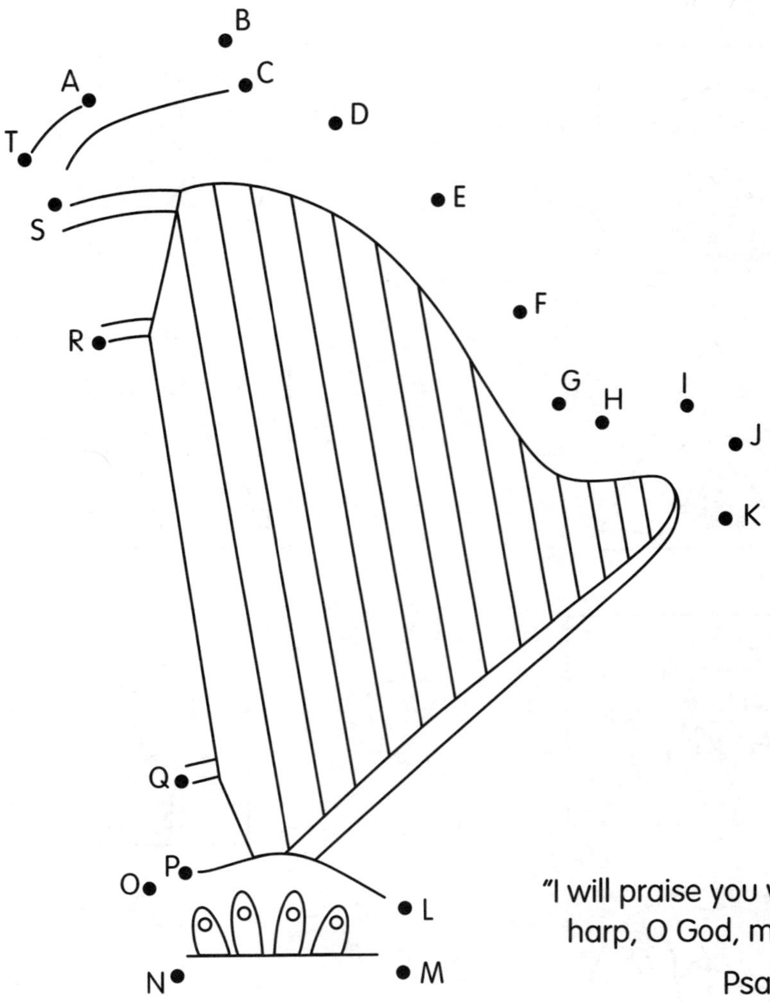

"I will praise you with the harp, O God, my God."
Psalm 43:4

GROWING IN GRACE

TALKING TO GOD
1 Thessalonians 5:17

You can talk to God anywhere. Find your way through the maze to see the places where this child talks to God. Write the letters you find along the way on the lines below.

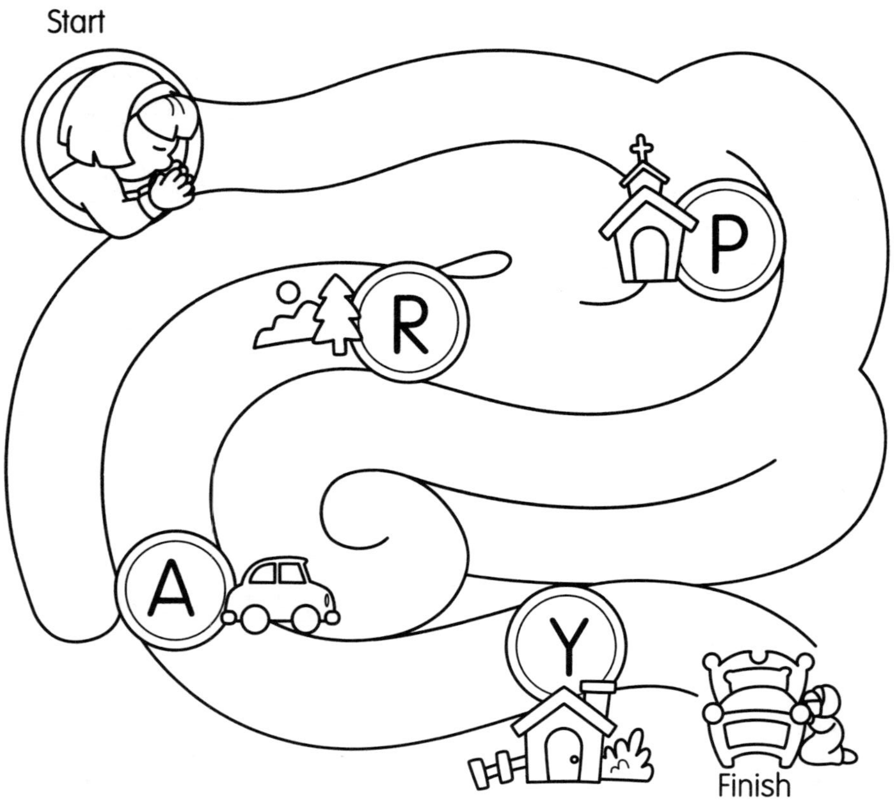

Start

Finish

___ ___ ___ ___ ___

WE TALK TO GOD WHEN WE PRAY.

Help draw the praying hands. Trace the dotted lines and color the words below.

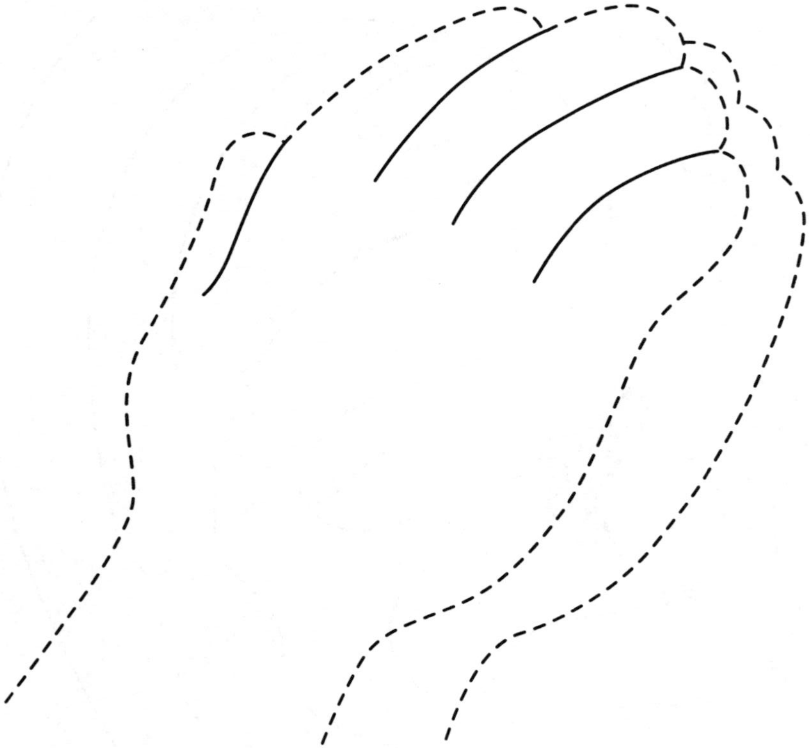

PRAY ALWAYS

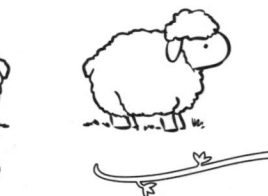

GOD WANTS US TO TALK TO HIM ALL OF THE TIME.

Where is your favorite place to pray? Draw a picture of yourself praying there in the space below.

GOD ALWAYS HEARS YOU.

Find your way through the maze. Remember that God is always ready to listen to you.

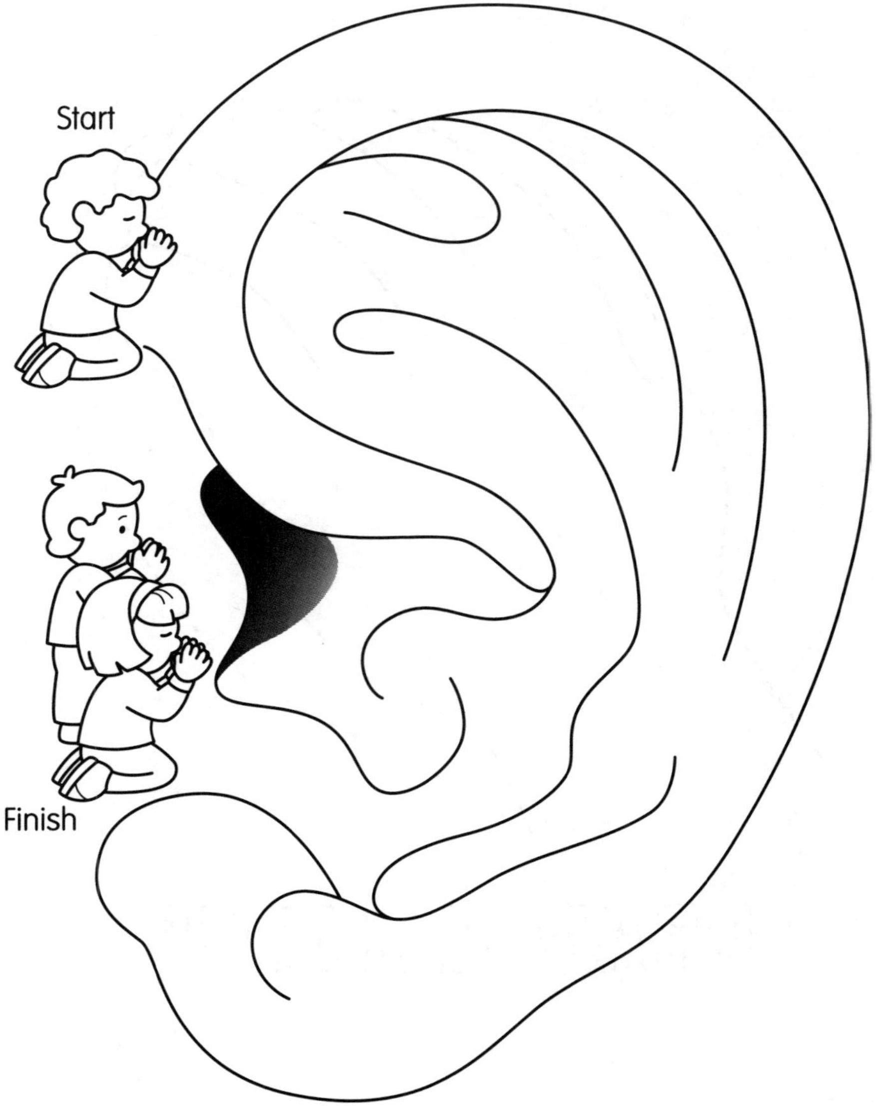

Start

Finish

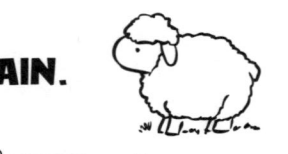

GROWING IN GRACE

THE ALPHA AND OMEGA
Revelation 1:8 NLT

Match the letters with the numbers. Then, write the letters on the lines to see what Alpha and Omega means.

"I am the Alpha and the Omega—

__ __ __ __   __ __ __   __ __ __
4 1 2 5   8 9 1   3 3 5 3 2

__ __ __   __ __ __,"
7 3 6   1 3 6

says the Lord God.

E	G	N	B	I	D	A	T	H
1	2	3	4	5	6	7	8	9

© Carson-Dellosa   Growing in Grace Children's Bulletins • CD-204028

JESUS WILL RETURN AGAIN.

Fill in the blanks below with the letter O to read who Jesus says He is.

"I am wh___ is still t___ c___me."

11

JESUS IS THE ALMIGHTY ONE.

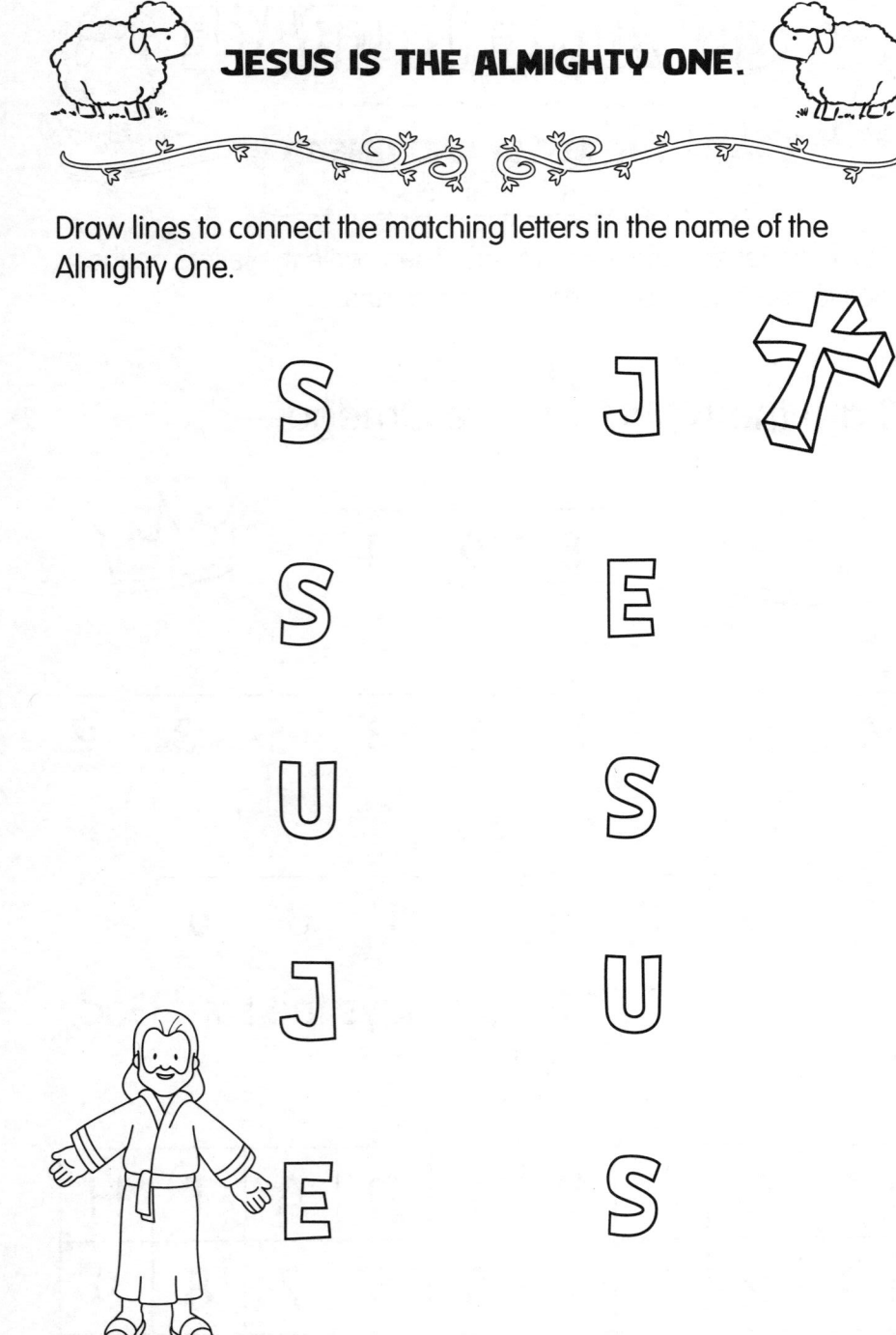

Draw lines to connect the matching letters in the name of the Almighty One.

S S U J S
E J U S E

GOD IS THE ALPHA AND OMEGA.

Find and circle the words *Alpha* and *Omega* three times each.

O M E G A A O
M A L P H A M
E E L A G P E
G G P O A H G
A A L P H A A
O E A L P H A

11